10652413

CHASING BUTTERFLIES

The True Story of a Daughter of 9/11

Ashley Bisman

Stone Tiger Books, LLC

Copyright © 2021 Ashley Bisman

First published by Stone Tiger Books in 2021.

All rights reserved; no part of this publication may be reproduced, stored in a retrieval system, or transmitted in any form or by any means, electronic, mechanical, photocopying, recording, or otherwise without the prior written permission of the Publisher. This book may not be lent, resold or otherwise disposed of by way of trade in any form of binding or cover other than that in which it is published, without the prior written consent of the Publisher.

Copyright © Ashley Bisman 2021

Cover and Jacket design by Rob Carter

ISBN: 9781735667669
eISBN: 9781735667676

Stone Tiger Books
225 E. 35th Street, Ground Fl.
New York, NY 10016

For Jade, Austin, and Eric. I love you.

CONTENTS

PROLOGUE

The fog obscuring the boat window couldn't shield me from the nightmare. I stared in shock as the Hudson River met land—what was left of it. Framed by waves and black sky, the Twin Towers had collapsed days earlier, and smoke was still wafting into the air. I was sixteen years old but felt like a little girl, my head resting on my mother's shoulders, in need of comfort and reassurance that I was safe. Our bodies swayed from side to side, flowing with the current. My surroundings appeared in shades of black and white, as if in an old film, just like the memories of my dad, Jeffrey Goldflam, already becoming fuzzy and distant.

I can't recall who arranged the ferries or where we departed from. It would be impossible to recollect the infinite details of this day. Why did my family accept this round-trip ticket to hell? Would I ever really know if my dad was up in his office or in the lobby that day? No. But at least I could visit the last spot his beautiful heart was and maybe, just maybe, take a part of his soul home with me. One less piece of him to remain in that pit.

On the ferry, men, women, and children sat side by side, shoulders brushing up against one another. The seats were narrow, creating an intimacy between us strangers. The swishing of the ocean against the hull of the boat was a reprieve from teardrops, pain, and sorrow. Coming from the families of lost loved ones, each lament had a distinctive sound. A sudden shriek would jolt me, a widow screaming at the top of her lungs, realizing she would never see her husband again. A child wailed when the adult next to him told him where mommy is—or, was.

Red Cross workers sat everywhere but said nothing. What were we to them? It was a spectacle that I was somehow ashamed to be a part of. I felt like an alien, a shell of the person I had been such a short time ago. No one could think. Trying to produce a sentence would have required too much physical strength, so nothing was said at all.

Wasn't it only yesterday that I had seen the looming buildings up close for the first time? It's as if I can still hear the plastic soles of my white Mary Janes clacking against the cobblestone roads of the South Street Seaport, my small steps outlining my father's much larger movements. He would hold my hand tight as we walked to his office.

As I sat on the boat, I lifted my head from my mother's arms and stared up at her. A true beauty, her olive skin complemented the copper tones of her hair and her chocolate-brown eyes. People always thought she was European because there was a grace to her movements, a charm that couldn't be taught. Her crisp white T-shirt was tucked into faded blue jeans gracing her hourglass figure, and I don't think I've ever seen anyone more beautiful, even at a time like this. But I also saw the tension beginning to overrun her face. Her mouth and jowls were clenched. Grinding teeth wrestled behind her stressed jawline. My mom sat frozen, taking in the sight of the people around her, all struggling to keep it together.

This paralyzed look was new to me. It made the skin on my arms and neck begin to tingle. In that moment, I knew she would never be the same. "Mom, why do we have to take a boat here?"

Her body inched closer to mine. "No one in New York City can get below 14th Street. It's completely closed off, sweetie."

"I don't want to go!"

With one stern look, I was put back in my place. As we docked, a loud voice echoed against the walls from a loudspeaker above: directions to move forward, instructions to disembark. But passengers continued sitting, none of us in a rush to see what came next. Volunteers in yellow vests scurried through the aisles, reaching out a helping hand, kindly guiding patrons up from their seats. My mom and brother stood in unison, and we tiptoed over the rocking platform. The humidity swept across my face. The hum of the engine became quiet, and a short dock stretched out ahead, possibly built for this very visit.

As we exited and embarked on unknown terrain, the smell of

salt water filled my nose, but it seemed different than usual. Very little was visible: a long walkway, maybe a hundred feet, which led to the epicenter of the rubble. As families proceeded forward on the trail, ash swirled in the air, dark and heavy. I unzipped the light jacket around my chest. The heat from the soot wounded us more than we already were. The draft felt so thick that each breath made me cough and gag. The normally noisy and bustling Battery Park City had been reduced to a battleground.

I drifted through a cloud of embers and smoke. I followed closely behind my brother, terrified of losing another person I loved. This was supposed to be the beginning of his senior year at college. Instead, he was here, trying to be strong for my mother and me.

As we approached some steps, I clenched a rough timber banister. Small splinters pricked my hands. One after another, my feet climbed. The altitude felt different, becoming even more muggy. When I reached the top, a large stage was before me, wide enough for visitors to fully view the destruction. The platform was void of cameras, news crews, and distractions. Standing here was the closest any of us would have to a funeral. This was our final goodbye, and it wasn't fair. It wasn't peaceful or religious. We didn't have our extended family or friends by our sides. Rather, this moment was inhumane—a wife or child should never have to say goodbye this way to someone they love.

The area was completely ours, but the view from these seats was scarring. I turned my head in slow motion, afraid to see the truth. Wreckage stretched endlessly, an avalanche of debris piled to the heavens. The ground where Tower 1 once rose was now post-war apocalyptic, everything in its way obliterated.

Mountains of metal and rubble created a graveyard. Penetrating from the remnants were steel beams, once part of the Towers reaching a thousand feet high. Now the structure appeared to be barely holding on. Firefighters wearing hard hats and masks dug as sweat dripped down their faces. The workers tread the accumulation of debris carefully, in search of victims' remains. I saw ironworkers, asbestos technicians, and structural engineers. It was impossible to know exactly which role each individual played. I heard talk about odors erupting from the pile, created by human decay.

I looked up at my brother, my eyes burning from the dirty air. "How did this happen days ago and there's still fire?"

He said nothing and continued to gaze blankly ahead.

Peering through the smoke, I could see a huge American flag waving in the breeze. The fabric floated effortlessly in the wind, so free. I felt anything but, chains on my ankles forcing me to stay and continue to watch a tragedy unfold. Soldiers, perfectly aligned, held hands up to their brows, saluting us—the wounded families.

Song lyrics began to creep into my head. A tune that had played in the background as I sat with my father just days ago, the melody replaying like a broken record: *Are you really what you dream?* My fists tightened, and I became angry, wishing this was all a nightmare that I could soon wake up from. Large excavators and tractors invaded the sacred space of Ground Zero. Workers picked up fragments of what once was and continued searching for the deceased.

1

Can't Live with Him,
Can't Live without Him

Eight years later, it's 2009, and lights from the construction of the Freedom Tower glisten through the windows. This allows me to appreciate every hard curve of his body. It's hot, and my heart beats wildly. I'm wrapped up in the sheets of a king-size bed, thirty stories high in a sleek studio loft in downtown Manhattan. Buildings shine against the night sky, creating an array of colors that hit my body perfectly, highlighting porcelain skin and blonde hair. It's just the two of us, romantic lovers for the night, full of intense passion and convenient chemistry. I'm so thankful he doesn't have roommates to help afford the New York City rent, as most people do. Of course, I know he isn't the one—the man I'll end up marrying, having children with, and living happily ever after with.

Most of my friends are in serious relationships, and the stress is building in the race for love and marriage. Meanwhile, I'm stuck in a metropolitan dating pool, which is turning out to be a revolving door of limited, unsatisfying possibilities. Still, being here is so much better than being alone. His arms are warm, and just for the night, I can make-believe this is it. I can languish in that fantasy before the sun comes up. So I close my eyes and nestle my head into a small space against his chest, where I inhale his sweet cologne and begin to fall asleep.

Hours later, my light blue eyes blink and struggle to adapt to the morning light. The ear-splitting sound of heavy machinery infiltrates the apartment. I jump up in shock: Am I late for work? What time is it? My dainty, red-polished nails press against my face as I wipe the sleep away. My body grazes his, leaning over, ever so gently, trying not to wake him. Beyond the lavish goose down pillows and Ralph Lauren bedding, his apartment looks different in the light of day. Dirty dishes lie in the sink, and the musty smell of unwashed laundry lingers in the air. The once-beautiful, white, crisp linen sheets are stained, tainted by sweat and reality. The beautiful facade of the night before has disappeared.

What was I thinking?

What was I drinking?

I have to get out without waking him. I roll out of bed and walk my nude self to the bathroom. Splashing water on my face, I stare into the reflection of the mirrored cabinet. I throw my blonde hair back in a ponytail. Good luck telling my girlfriends about this one. I take one last glance, trying to wipe smeared makeup off of my cheeks. One quick peek in the medicine cabinet to see if I'll find something interesting about this new conquest. Maybe a prescription bottle revealing his Adderall addiction or a mental health disorder? An ointment for his STD? I sure hope not.

The only thing worth remembering is his Armani cologne, which I spritz in the air, wave my hand through, and breathe in. I take in every last scent of his aroma and the perfection of yesterday evening. I throw my bra into my bag, grab some of his clothes (squeezing into my skinny jeans from last night seems impossible right now), and hustle out the front door.

I approach the elevator and wait as my heart begins to pound. As I step into the small rectangular space, I feel lucky to be alone. I stare at the screen as red numbers light up: 30, 29, 28, 27, 26. As I descend, I can't help but think, was my dad in the elevator when it happened? Or did he try to take the stairs, a place I wish I was right now instead of this metal box? It can't be moving any slower. The walls seem as if they're going to close in on me when suddenly there's a stop at 25. My stomach lurches for a second as a couple in their mid-thirties enters and looks me up and down. They give each other a quick smile as their backs turn toward me. I am oh-so-mortified. They're impeccably dressed and giving me that shameful nod. They look back from time to time, those icky, judgy eyes, the ones that can't help themselves from speaking.

"Oh, I feel so sorry for you," they seem to say. "You're still in that phase of your life? Well, good luck to you. Seems like you'll need it."

How are we only on the fifteenth floor?

I can't bear any more stares or humiliation, let alone the claustrophobia. I hold my breath, as if that will help. I hate being this high up in the air, moving way too slowly, with no control whatsoever. Finally, the elevator opens, and I exhale in relief.

As I pass through the lobby doors, the sun hits my face, and I look up into the very early morning sky. The air feels refreshing against my skin, which is still in last night's makeup. I dart down the street, looking down and praying that I don't run into anyone I know: Ashley! What a surprise! What are you doing here so early in the morning, and whose clothes are you wearing?

My eyeliner has migrated to my cheekbones. The foundation, which was once smooth and creamy beige, is now rubbed off, revealing little freckles on my nose and forehead. My hair is up on the top of my head in a librarian-like bun with loose strands rebounding against the side of my face. Pointy stilettos with red-bottomed soles are in one hand, while the other holds up the guy's shorts, two sizes too big and dangling from my body. Construction workers howl and whistle. They can't get enough of my stride down the runway, or in this case, Washington Street in Tribeca. I walk by the construction site of One World Trade Center, and the workers stare at me, call out pickup lines, their phone numbers, marital status—anything to get a date or, at the very least, some attention. I'm embarrassed and parade on, understanding that this is well deserved and what one gets after the escapades, or sexcapades, to be blunt, from the previous night. I dash to the subway with one hand trying to cover my face, as if these guys might recognize me. I wonder, *What would Dad think of me?*

I ride the subway north, up to my apartment. The stench of stale beer and urine stings my nose. The late-night party animals taking the train home certainly knew how to mark their territory: welcome to Manhattan. But then a smile breaks across my face, and I can't help but giggle as I reminisce about last night.

"23rd Street station! 23rd Street!" The voice of a conductor, muffled and staticky, interrupts my reverie. A loud ding sounds through the train car, and the metal doors begin to close. Alarm seizes me, and I leap forward, reminded of where I am. My body lunges, rushing toward the sliding doors. Passengers look on, wondering if the daydreamer will make it. Suddenly, I feel an intense pressure on the lower half of my body, and I'm unable to move. My face grows red with mortification and sheer embarrassment.

"Lady, hey, lady!" a man yells in my direction. The thick black frames of his glasses complement his similar-toned fedora, tilted to one side. "Your butt's stuck in the doors! That's what happens when ya don't pay attention."

An elderly woman sits beside him, slowly craning her neck. A cane trembles beneath her fingertips as she clutches for balance. Her voice is low and frail. "Why isn't the train moving? What's going on?"

"What are ya, blind or somethin'? That girl almost missed her stop and now she's stuck in the doors! Now we all gonna be late for work. Maybe if her booty wasn't so big, she would have made it."

As the staring eyes trace my body, roaming south, the irritation becomes more painful. Gaping onlookers are burning holes right through me. The train doors open and close on my butt several times and finally, like an animal let off of its leash, I'm able to run free.

I rush into my apartment and fling my bag behind me. I kick my feet and shake my ankles as the stilettos fly across the entryway of my small studio. The heels land on the linoleum floor of the kitchen. There isn't much space in my five-hundred-square-foot oasis, dominated as it is by the modern white Crate and Barrel shelves my mom bought as a housewarming gift when I rented my first apartment in Manhattan. As is often the case, my face drops until I see a familiar silver picture frame on the bottom shelf, a few inches above the wood floor.

The crystal blue eyes of my father in this five-by-seven photograph call out to me, to my matching pair, catching me in their grasp and not letting go. This picture was taken several months before he was killed. He had landed a new job as the CFO of Cantor Fitzgerald. It was a well-respected and coveted position. He had been working there almost a year to the day.

The headshot captured him perfectly. He looks the part of an intelligent businessman, with his crisp white button-down shirt and black suit jacket outlining his broad shoulders. His thick head of brown hair is perfect, with each strand in place, and his pale, white skin makes his lips seem redder and his eyes bluer. He was successful, however one might measure that. He finally had the dream job that would allow him to retire young and spend more time with his family, primarily his high school sweetheart, who had become his wife, and their two children—one of them me. When he stared into the lens of the camera that day, he had no clue that these dreams would never actually happen. It was as if his company had known that the faces of their employees would not remain vibrant and full of life forever. This was a moment in time when my dad was working, thriving, and happy. Now, as his crystal blue eyes meet mine, I stare into the past and remember a simple time when I was little, holding his hands as they lifted me up above the waves in Montauk, far away on the tip of Long Island.

The ocean was overwhelming, intimidating. The endless tides would come crashing down from double my height. The Montauk surf felt refreshing on my skin, splashing against me as the August sun beat down on us.

"Ashkappash," my father would say, "don't let go of my hand."

He smiled down at me, a small child at the time, and held tight as the current sucked our feet deeper into the sand. Then another ripple formed, and it crashed in larger than the last. I looked up at him, wearing his aviator sunglasses that reflected the harsh sun.

"Daddy, I'm scared."

My knees, cold and wet, were shaking. Just as a huge wave came crashing toward us, my arms flew into the air, holding his hands as I was lifted up over the breaking tide. He swept me up into his arms, and I pressed my face against his chest, the salt water from his skin on my lips. The light hair on his chest tickled my nose, and I looked up at him and smiled.

"Baby girl," he said, wiping the sand off my cheek. "I'll always protect you."

I notice the time and brush away the memory, like the sand from the ocean off my face. I blink away the sadness as a few salty tears hit my lips. It's as if I can still taste that day back in Montauk. I take a deep breath. It's almost time for work, but first a quick run.

I do this every morning before I leave. I throw my hair back in a ponytail and don't bother to wash my face. I grab a pair of tight black Capri workout pants and slide them on over the lace Hanky Panky thong I slept in by mistake. I slip into a pink sports bra and tank top, which match my sneakers perfectly. I take a look in the mirror. My eyes are brighter than usual, which happens when I get sad. Still, I smile at myself. It's a new day, a new time, a new chapter.

As I lace up my Reeboks, I pick up the loose-fitting T-shirt I wore home and hold it up to my nose. The smell of men's cologne fills my nostrils, and I inhale. I close my eyes and think back to the magnificence of last night. I take the shirt and toss it over my shoulders, where it finds its final resting place on the bed. I head out to take my early morning run.

I head toward the river, where a keen view of Lower Manhattan rests along the horizon. My feet sweep across the pavement, and my breathing becomes deeper. I push myself to go faster, my ponytail swinging back and forth. I need to shake off last night. Living in Chelsea has its perks, but there is a downside: most of the men here are gay, which makes it impossible to meet an eligible guy, at least in my immediate neighborhood. But I'm close to the West Side Highway, which has the best running paths in all of Manhattan. I run downtown, with the water to my right and luxurious apartment buildings to my left. The skyscrapers of Battery Park City lay ahead of me, and as I inch closer and closer, I pick up my pace. The Statue of Liberty appears small at first but becomes clearer as I make progress and gain speed. It's pretty quiet this time of day. Joggers and bikers appear like occasional drops of rain on a summer day. At times, I'll pass a cute guy running alongside me. If I'm lucky he'll have his shirt off and have a rocking body; some eye candy during a workout never hurt anybody. Still, it frustrates me to run by an attractive man and know I'll never see him again. In those moments, I tease myself, I wish I could wear my cell phone number on the back of my workout shirts! Then, as I pass the West Village and get closer to the construction of the Freedom Tower, my heart pounds harder, and my anxiety rises. My stomach begins to ache, and any appetite I had has now been lost.

I pray today isn't going to be *that kind of day*, another heart-wrenching morning where I miss my dad so much that it hurts. As if someone is squeezing me, and it feels like I'm about to burst. But I'm not going to think about my fears and anxieties from the past. I keep running.

It's been almost a decade since the night terrors, the post-9/11 dreams where my dad was murdered. They would take over my body as I slept, holding me hostage and making me relive the moment over and over, bringing me back to a sense of helpless despair. I would wake up and my pajamas would be drenched in a pool of sweat. The bitter stench would reach my nose, and I'd look down to see my chest and palms dripping and hot. I'd inhale slowly and breathe out a huge puff of air and a sigh of relief. Every so often, this would all happen again. It is as if there is a ghost, an evil monster reminding me that even though time has passed, the painful memories would never go away. The glass, metal, dust, and piles of rubble have never been fully cleaned up in the depths of my mind. There those vivid images live, waiting quietly and patiently. Then just when I least expect it, they appear again. Each nightmare is worse than the one before, one-upping the other as if stuck in a mean game of chess. I'd like to think those days are fully over. I need to get home. I have to be at work in less than an hour.

And I have to move on with my life.

How much longer can I go on like this? Reliving 9/11 in my mind. Trying to find Mr. Right. When will life simply just come together? How long will it actually take to find the man of my dreams? Have I already dated him, my "happily-ever-after"? Have we already met, and I stupidly dumped him or didn't give him a fair chance? Even if I had found my Prince Charming, would that be enough? Would that fulfill me?

Deep in the pit of my stomach a tension forms, a knot that becomes larger and spreads to my chest, the heavy pressure resting near my ribs. I think I have the answers but choose to keep them buried so far into the abyss, certain they will never see the light of day. After all, isn't there a get-out-of-jail-free card? Once you experience one tragedy, don't you get a free pass from the rest? In my heart I know that's not how the world works, but for now, I can pretend.

2

And Then He Was Gone

Τhe ding of the school bell echoes in my ears and it's a relief to have made it to work on time. The boom of the wooden classroom door against the cinderblock wall indicates the time, barely 8:03 in the morning. The students dart inside like bats out of hell. I sit behind my desk on the uncomfortable wooden chair provided by the New York City Department of Education, sipping some much-needed coffee. Pretending to look through my lesson plans for the day, I hope the caffeine kicks in fast. I take long, slow sips of the hot liquid and close my eyes, inhaling the hazelnut smell.

The zoo-like ramblings of my students are the sudden news flashes that I'm responsible for these thirty ten-year-olds. The children scurry to their desks, and I'm reminded that the future of America is depending on me to lead the way: a young, single, bar-hopping, friends-and-shopping, slightly hungover teacher.

The pitter-patter of fifth-grade feet encourages me to gulp down a couple of Advil before it's too late. "Good morning, Ms. Goldflam," says the chorus of high-pitched voices, cranking up the decibels in record time.

"Ms. Goldflam, your face looks funny. Are you tired today?"

The sounds I normally love have become too loud.

"Ms. Goldflam, why does your hair smell so weird?"

My body twists—little Salwa is playing with my ponytail, taking the long strands and holding them up to her nose. Good god! I don't need this kid inhaling my dirty do's and dont's of last night.

My hand pats Salwa's back. "Please take your seat, sweetheart, thank you." In other words, I've been caressed enough in the past twelve hours. Get your hands out of my hair!

All ranked within the ninety-ninth percentile of the Stanford-Binet IQ Test, my students are in the Gifted and Talented program. Some people ask if I'm gifted or have special talents. The answer is no, but I've managed to do the job well, according to my students, their parents, and the school administration. As it turns out, although a ten-year-old may be gifted, he or she still picks their nose, tattles, and has trouble zipping up a jacket—just like any ordinary child.

Silence fills the air as the students' eyes study the workbooks in front of them. The kneading of erasers against loose-leaf brings a rubbery scent to the air. There's a nostalgic tune of fingers tapping against desks, but this rhythm, in this classroom silence, while the thoughts of Dad on *that kind of day* linger, brings me back to my days as a student, not so very long ago.

Mr. Smith's Class, September 11, 2001 was written in messy white chalk along the top of the blackboard. I had understood the date being up there, but why the instructor's name? We were sixteen years old, perfectly capable of remembering who our social studies instructor was. Rows of desks were filled with friends, boys and girls I had known all my life. As juniors in high school, we were daydreaming about our futures and final freedom from this room. I looked up at the instructor, who appeared to be in his early thirties. Even if I had been of age, he wasn't attractive or like someone I would ever hope to date. He had a glimpse of potential, though. Maybe cute when he was younger, a nerdy history enthusiast with academic sex appeal. Unfortunately, this look did not grow with him. He must have been single, as he wasn't wearing a wedding ring. His pants hung about two inches too long, gathering at the top of his shoelaces. The tucked-in shirt hitting his lanky chest was stained, and his voice echoed off the walls and through my ears.

The colorful tattoos on the arm of the rebel next to me provided excellent reading material to distract me from the boredom. His jet-black hair landed below his ears, slicked down by a dark headset which thumped a familiar song from Blink-182. Beyond the light punk rock music, whispers grew into chatter. The room had become filled with echoes of key words: World Trade Center, airplanes, fire.

"Ashley, Ashley, over here!" I turned around to see Jill, her long brown hair outlining her round face, accentuating high cheekbones. We had met at our fifth-grade school picnic and had been inseparable ever since. Her voice was shaky. "People are saying that an airplane crashed into the Twin Towers. Is this true? Do you know what's going on?" The question sounded absurd, impossible.

"It has to be a rumor," I assured her. "I mean, that's ridiculous."

I sat completely still, paralyzed. Was it possible that this could have actually happened? Seconds went by, then minutes, until my stomach ached. It was then that I knew the truth in my gut. An instinctive feeling took over my body, an alarm with sirens so loud that I was brought to my feet.

"Ms. Goldflam, we aren't finished here," the teacher scolded. "Please sit down."

I felt like a deer blinded by headlights, knowing it was about to get run over. I didn't realize that a pencil was still in my hand when it suddenly dropped to the floor and rolled backward, bringing all eyes in the room in my direction. The instructor waited for me to push my chair in. Classmates gawked, waiting to see if I would obey the command. Memories played in my mind: my dad's picture-perfect Mona Lisa smile, soft brown hair, that sweet smell of breath mints, and those tall buildings.

The soles of my Converse sneakers squeaked against the tiled floor. I sprinted as the classroom door slammed behind me. The chaos of the moment had made the long, narrow hallway seem never-ending as I ran. I could have sworn I was hearing my heart as it pounded frantically in my chest. Students and teachers began pouring out of classrooms, lining up against the corridors. Each person was immobile, as if posing in a picture hanging on the wall; they had no life, no ability to reach out and help. Their stares felt like bullets, piercing holes into my skin.

I turned a corner to find the main office, lit up by a bright television hanging on the wall. As I rushed inside, the image on the screen seeped out, grabbing my throat and squeezing it tight. My lungs struggled to take in air as I watched the top of Tower 1, black and burning. Enormous clouds of smoke engulfed the skyscraper as wild red and orange flames burst in the sky. There was footage of people running in the street, as if they were about to be swallowed whole by the debris. That's where my dad was, on the 101st floor of Tower 1.

Back in my classroom in Queens, the bellow of the loudspeaker brings me back to reality. I'm compelled to check my students' work for reassurance of the year: yes, it's 2009. I'm now a teacher, these are my students, and I will make them feel safe. More secure than I felt on that day many years ago. The short mental pep talk lifts my spirits, and just as I'm about to get the children's attention, I notice that the middle button on my shirt is undone. I'm a mess. Thanks to a certain someone and our friend Jack (as in Daniels), I'm forced to make a quick wardrobe adjustment.

"Ms. Goldflam, I can see your bra!"

A melody of giggles chimes through the classroom, and I clap my hands to get attention. "Boys and girls, today's going to be exciting. It's read-aloud-with-friends day! Can someone explain what this means?"

Samit, in the front row, raises his hand, waving it back and forth. His interest in the event is sweet and a nice change from others who stare up at the ceiling, caring less. He stands up when he speaks, commanding the attention of his peers. "It's when your family members come into class and bring one of their favorite stories to read to everyone."

Exaggerated squeals of thrill ring in the air as Salwa yells out, "It's my dad! There he is, through the window!" The students stand up behind their desks, on tiptoe, trying to peek. I've never met Salwa's father, but we have spoken over the phone several times to discuss his daughter's progress.

My fingers rub the temples of my head in a clockwise motion. The thought of having to be professional and charming with a parent right now is exhausting. "Salwa, please greet your dad and show him in."

My eyes dart upward and find a hot man standing in front of the Smartboard. He's wearing a black suit, dress pants, and a button-down blue-and-white-striped shirt. The top button is undone, and his sleeves are rolled just above his wrists, revealing a silver watch and fingers with no jewelry—wedding band non-existent. His hair is perfectly slicked back off of his face, which enhances his chiseled nose and soft pink lips.

My fingers work quickly, tying the bottom of my loose-fitting shirt in a cute knot, showing just a little skin by my stomach. I pull at my hair, tearing my ponytail out and letting the long waves fall down my arms. A cheap Loreal lip gloss purchased at CVS rolls forward as I pull the front drawer of my desk open. I apply the shade quickly, pressing my lips together, feeling the shimmery pink liquid sink into my skin.

I strut across the classroom in a sultry motion and hold out my manicured fingernails.

"Hi! I'm Salwa's teacher, it's such a pleasure to finally meet you!" My smile is innocent yet flirty. Will he get the hint? His strong grip embraces mine.

"I'm Sam, as you know, Salwa's dad. Great to meet you. I wish I could have made an appearance earlier in the year. Better late than never, I guess." He blushes. Our fingers linger in an extremely long handshake. Smiling, I pull the loose strands of hair falling across my face, gently placing them behind my ear. "Please begin when you're ready." Sam stares at the roomful of youngsters, scanning for a familiar face, his daughter. His fingers slowly unzip his messenger bag, and the procrastination leads me to believe that he is nervous.

"Hi, class! Today I have two stories that I would like to share. Do you have any questions before I begin?"

Rookie mistake. Never ask a room full of children if they have questions. You'll be lucky if you make it out of there before your ninetieth birthday.

"Hands down, everybody," I chime in. "Let's see what you'll be learning about, and then we can answer questions at the end." Sam sends a thankful smile in my direction, knowing he's been saved from a firing squad of inquiries.

Then he holds a book in the air. "I picked out this story because I moved to New York City from Bangladesh when I was a child. It's important to know about the history of the country you live in." His posture straightens, and his bold voice begins to gain confidence. His body glides with ease while he brings the book close to each child. Their faces turn, traveling with the colors of the cover illustration as it moves past.

The title is *What Were the Twin Towers?* An extra-large picture of the World Trade Center is on the cover with a little boy staring up at the buildings.

Particles of coffee spray from my mouth and the plastic cup tips over. The brown liquid spreads in a furious motion, consuming my desk. Giggles fill the air as I blot my lesson plan book with tissues.

"Excuse me, Sam?" He stares, chuckling while I clean the spill. "Can you please read a different book? I had planned on reading that to the class on another day." The lie easily slips off of my tongue. I know that would never happen. Although 9/11 was eight years ago, the thought of teaching it to a class full of children breaks my heart.

Sam gives a quick nod and places his next book on a pedestal for the children to see. "Can someone tell me what they learn from the cover art?"

The students raise their hands, each child completely entrenched in the lesson. Farhat says, "The title reads *September Roses*, and I see buildings that are the Twin Towers with flowers floating above in the sky."

"Very good." Sam grins, relieved that the class is so interested.

Sam and the children continue talking, and I pull at the cloth of my top, becoming hot. Will there ever come a day when 9/11 won't be mentioned? Will the Earth spin a full rotation without me hearing that date or the words of Towers and terror? How is it possible to remain a sane person with the constant reminder of how I lost my dad?

I don't want to interrupt but also can't bear to listen. My students don't know about my past. It's a secret I keep, among others. Why should complete strangers and acquaintances know such a personal detail about my life? This information has to be earned, given as a token when I know I can trust. 9/11, a day shared with the entire world, leaves nowhere for me to hide. Now I need to take back some of that control.

My eyes meet Sam's, ditching the flirtatious batting of eyelashes. Luckily, I'm able to get his attention. Clearly, he's my soulmate, receiving the hint loud and clear that I don't want books about 9/11 read in class. He gives a thoughtful, apologetic nod and spends the remainder of his time having children pick out stories from our class library, all pre-screened and approved by me before the first day of school. My back and shoulders ease, lowering in relief. Now I can go back to recovering from my hangover while the students hear tales of lions, witches, and wardrobes.

All too soon there's an uproar of clapping, and I look up to see that Sam has packed up and is ready to hit the road. I leap forward to catch him. "Let me walk you out! Kids, please take out your journals and write down any questions, comments, or thoughts you have about the presentation. We will go over this in a few minutes."

The children race to dig up their marble-patterned notebooks from mostly messy desks. The girls take out pink pens with sparkly designs, while the boys opt for standard blue or black ink. Other teachers in the school make their students use pencil.

I've never cared about small things like that. If a child loves to write, who cares what they write with?

The breeze from the hallway hits my face and Sam turns toward me. "Ms. Goldflam, Ashley, this was fun." His fingertips dance along the tips of his pockets, and the jingling of loose change awakens me, realizing he's waiting for a response.

My pale complexion takes on the color of freshly picked roses. "It was! I look forward to our next parent-teacher conference; hopefully you can attend in person next time."

Sam walks away and then, just before turning the corner, spins around.

This is all the confirmation I need. A feeling of confidence takes over, and I shout, "My phone number's in the school roster!"

Will a date with one of my students' parents get me into trouble with the principal? Good question, but I couldn't care less.

3

Welcome to the Race

I squint in the glare from the sun as I enter my apartment. A peaceful mood is created by the pink-and-yellow horizon. My hands pull at the tight fabric of my jeans, tossing them off in record speed. Plush flannel brushes along my legs, a keepsake from an ex-boyfriend. I shimmy a gray hoodie over my head and fall to the center of my Macy's microfiber couch. I push the remote buttons, flipping through channels until I land on Sex and the City, my all-time favorite. Carrie has just had secret sex with Mr. Big. I cuddle underneath a soft blanket, holding a bowl of popcorn, tossing a few pieces into my mouth on commercial breaks.

The phone starts to ring. Do I, or do I not, pick up? It's probably one of my girlfriends calling to talk about guy problems. As the tune from my cell continues, it's beginning to interrupt the evening. I begin to wonder who it could be. Maybe it's Sam, the cute dad I met today at work?

My issue with phone calls is that I never know what's on the other end: once I answer, I may hear something devastating, news that has the potential to change my life forever. A ringing phone evokes in me, for example, the dozens of calls and texts I receive annually on 9/11 or Father's Day. Friends thinking that because it's a certain day of the year I should be distraught. Little do they know, missing a loved one doesn't revolve around a calendar. And loss can occur in a moment, like on a Tuesday back in 2001.

News of the airplanes hitting the Towers was widespread, and I couldn't get out of school. I had no driver's license and had to beg every administrator to let me go. Finally, the guidance counselor offered a ride.

In his green Toyota Camry, we pulled up the hill of my driveway. It was the place I was born, and those walls held the brightest and darkest secrets of my past. The stick shift hadn't yet been geared to park, but my passenger door was already open. I flew toward the garage door as it creaked upward. My body was tingling, itching to get past the barricade. My father's bright red sports car was parked ahead. It was his most prized possession, and in this moment had a life of its own: it, too, was waiting for him to come home. I raced by the harsh reminder of my dad's absence and hiked up a flight of stairs. Loud voices echoed against the walls. My right foot hit the top step and I collided into a crowd of women; every friend of my mother's was in the room. This should have been a warning, giving me the heads-up that privacy was a privilege I would not see again for a long time.

The black leather couches in the den were filled with frightened soccer moms. Most were watching the news in horror, while others chose to stand in the corners, speculating about where my dad was and if he was okay. Leave it to the Jewish mothers of Long Island; nothing could make them speechless, not even this. They swarmed around my mom like angry bees, having been aggravated and torn away from their hive. The noise of their guessing games filled the air: "Was it a terrorist attack?" "Was it an accident, a plane crash?" "Was Jeff in the building?" The questions of the women were in tandem, and I couldn't figure out if they were speaking out of concern or gossip.

I shuffled through the smells of Dior perfume and acrylic nails. "Mom! Mom! I'm here!" I yelled, but she didn't hear me. I saw her body in the eye of the hurricane. So I pushed through and grabbed her.

She reached for my hand as if I were going to be brushed away by the chaos. Her arms closed in around me tightly, and I was finally at peace knowing we wouldn't be apart again. She scanned my body for bruises, signs of hurt—unable to believe that I could actually be standing here in one piece, because everything else in the world had fallen in shambles.

Her trembling fingers touched my cheek. "How did you get here? All of the schools are under lockdown. I didn't want to come get you because then I'd know that this was real."

"Mom, I told the principal about Dad. The teachers kept trying to calm me down, saying everything was all right. They asked what floor Daddy worked on, and I said 101. That's when I saw the panic on their faces, and they knew they had to take me home!"

She wiped her tears away and placed her fingers in between mine. A breath of relief left her body as the phone began to ring. A neighbor picked up and ran toward us, putting the receiver on speaker. My brother's voice was frantic on the other end. "Mom, I walked in from class and it was all over the news. Tower 1 just collapsed! I don't know what to do. I can't get out of Indiana; the airports are shut down."

My mom calmed her voice. "Honey, rent a car, do whatever you need to, just get here, and be safe."

She was trying to be strong, for all of us. But I could tell my presence here wasn't enough. I was too young, unable to totally take on this burden with her: she needed my brother.

"Don't worry," he said, sounding responsible and suddenly in control. "I'm on my way."

So that's when I learned a phone call is not just a phone call: there's a lack of control I don't like giving in to. Back on the couch, in the glare of my television, I stare at my cell phone as it continues to ring and am hesitant to answer. I had an awesome day, managing to overcome my bouts of sadness and a hangover while also flirting with a hot dad—can't I leave it at that? But then it suddenly becomes clear I need a distraction from the nightmare I just revisited in my mind.

I answer, lowering the volume as the percussion theme song from *Sex and the City* plays. In its place, shrieking screams scratch my eardrums as Brittney, my childhood friend, yells those two words that every friend dreads: "I'm engaged!"

These syllables smack me hard in the face. The popcorn goes flying, and I can feel all pressure points in my body pulsing. My heart skips a beat, as if something unimaginable just happened: my best friend got engaged before I did!

As I kneel down, trying to dig kernels out of my new shag rug, I try to ignore the jealous animal instinct that wants to climb through the phone, steal Brittney's ring, and fight to the death to take her place. Why should she have the rock on her hand first? How is it fair that she gets to go bridal gown shopping tomorrow? I imagine her curvy hourglass figure filling a sexy white mermaid dress. Her silky, dirty blonde hair graced with a lavish lace veil. I've striven for this moment longer; this should be me!

"Wow! Congratulations, Britt, I can't believe it!" She's been with her boyfriend Noah for six months; I've had cheap sweaters from Forever 21 that lasted longer. How could this have happened so quickly? "Tell me everything! I want to hear how he proposed!

What does your ring look like? Have you begun to think about bridesmaid dresses yet?" They will inevitably be pastel with an empire waist, causing every girl to look nine months pregnant.

Brittney says she will fill me in on the details later. She has to call more friends and spread the good news. As we hang up, a sudden pounding on the door brings me to my feet. The sound becomes intense, the banging growing louder with each second. Who is this psycho, and haven't they ever heard of a doorbell?

My hands fumble, struggling to turn the rusted bolt lock. Jill stands in the hall, her almond-shaped eyes wider than usual, in panic. She holds up a magnum bottle of red wine as a greeting. "Well that does it!" she yells, and I'm positive my neighbors and all of Manhattan can hear. Pushing her way inside, she shows herself to the kitchen. "We are going to be alone forever," she shouts, all while opening the cabinet above the sink and reaching for my fancy crystal wine glasses, an old engagement gift of my parents'.

I sarcastically grin. "Just help yourself. The plastic red solo cups would have done just fine." The situation seems to be right out of a funny movie. The tagline would read, "Distraught friend seeks drinking partner to ease her lonely soul."

Jill hands me a generous pour, and I take a big sip. "So I guess Brittney broke the news to you first?"

"Damn right she did." The intensity radiates as her thick brown hair begins to sway across her face. "And I'm happy for her, Ash, really, I am. But now I feel like we're on the clock, more than ever before."

We've all been there. News comes out about an engagement, and girls are expected to do what any nice, normal friend would do. Send a wedding gift? Yeah, right. Instead, Jill and I sit on the couch toe to toe, playing a game of footsie under a velvet blanket. Not because we want to, my sofa is just too small.

I lift up the pinot noir and refill Jill's glass. It's not completely empty, but I have a feeling she needs a second helping. As the trickling liquid splashes into her cup, I ask, "Why is it that we hit our mid-twenties and become obsessed with finding a husband and getting married?"

She chugs the beverage, swishing the alcohol around in her mouth. "I got that feeling when I was on the phone with Brittney. The devil on my shoulder that tells me I'll never get to wear a beautiful diamond ring or a fancy white wedding gown."

I sit up and pat Jill on the shoulder. "Congratulations, my friend. You are now part of the race."

She rolls her eyes. "Jeez, are you drunk already? What the heck are you talking about?"

Oh, sweet Jill. Innocent and kind Jill. "You have not been properly informed. Get your sports bra on and don't forget the Lululemon leggings, either. Lace up your Reeboks and sprint like there's a friends and family sale at Bloomingdale's. We are now part of the race for the ring."

Our eyes meet and we raise our glasses in unison. The dainty clink of the fine crystal acts as the horn blowing at the start of an Olympic marathon.

After an hour of drinking away our First-World problems and sorrows, Jill puts herself in a taxi home. My mind is filled with this concept of women all searching for Mr. Right. How come men never seem as eager to settle down?

Men enjoy the race too, but not for the ring. They're searching for hot twenty-something girls with perky boobs and a slim figure. There are no nuptials, no happy ending. Well, in their dreams I suppose there's a happy ending, but it's more hands-on. So where do we find the eligible bachelors? The ones who actually do want to put a ring on it?

What I know for sure is this: I'll never forget the day I began to dream of my hypothetical wedding. It was an illusion of elegance and grandeur, thanks to a conversation with my dad just a year before he died.

In the late nineties, retro trends from the sixties were so in. My dad waved his long fingers through the magenta fringes that hung down from my shawl. I was in a black tube top, which was very cool at the time, and a patterned geometric pencil skirt. We sat next to each other as our thumbs wrestled on the armrest in between us. It was my cousin Jamie's wedding day; she was marrying Ben, her high school sweetheart. As we sat waiting for the bride to come down the aisle, my dad and I did what we always do to pass time in temple: play thumb war. He would never let me win, his competitive edge taking hold with his fifteen-year-old daughter. "Ashkappash," he whispered at the end of one round, "you look hip tonight!"

As our fingers intertwined in another aggressive battle to take the other down, he took his other hand and threw it on top of mine. My thumb went sideways and lost once again. "Cherry bomb!" He laughed as his large hand pushed mine to the side.

"That's not fair, Dad, you cheated."

He shrugged his shoulders and took a deep breath. We watched as a groomsman and bridesmaid walked in, hand in hand. My cousin Sara appeared next, the bride's sister. She glided down the aisle alone, with a tear streaming down her face. She looked proud and sentimental.

My dad gazed at me as I sat staring at the white flowers and candles around the room. "What do you want your wedding day to be like?"

I had never thought about it before. Then, suddenly, images of pink flowers and raw silk linens came to mind. "I want . . ." But just as I began to answer, the large French doors opened, and my cousin entered the room, her white gown covered in crystal beads that shimmered with glowing silver. Her cathedral veil followed behind her as she held her dad's hand.

Jamie glided toward Ben, her soon-to-be husband. Her blue eyes and pink lips graced an angelic face as the ballgown hugged her small waist and extended outward, wrapping her in a fairy tale of chiffon and lace.

My dad nudged my shoulder. "One day that will be you." His proud eyes stared into mine, and a Mona Lisa smile came upon his face. He looked at me with complete love and adoration. As the ceremony continued, and the couple took their vows, I wondered: would a man ever be able to see me the way my father does?

"I now pronounce you Mr. and Mrs. Ben Goldstein!" The rabbi's voice was loud and celebratory. Clearly, he was just as happy to get to the cocktail hour as we were. There was applause and cheers of joy as the newlyweds raced down the aisle, heading toward their happily ever after.

On September 11, 2001, Ben Goldstein was killed in Tower 2 of the World Trade Center. He was twenty-six years old.

Really, I think to myself, curled on the couch with an empty pinot bottle, why get married at all? What's the point in trying to make a happy life if it's going to end in disaster? But this uncertainty doesn't put up a fight for long with life's other surprises, the good kinds: The electrifying feeling I get when I'm suddenly kissed. The touch of hands against my body. Soft breath against my ear as I hear "I love you" and get butterflies in my stomach. This is all the motivation I need, reminders of the moments worth living for. I refuse to be scared and give up.

4

Mr. K

Six months later, Brittney sits across from me at a luncheonette. My ears sting from the tapping of silverware and the surrounding clatter from the Sunday morning brunch crowd. My body squeaks against the rubbery green booth as I'm hypnotized by her engagement ring. Her left hand holds a fork that stabs at lettuce as she eats. The dreaded wedding diet. Brittney's eyes meet mine as she diverts from her salad. "David's just so square, Ash. What do you see in him?"

I laugh, appreciating her honesty. "He's good on paper: Jewish, attractive, lawyer. It checks all the boxes." A smile comes across my face as I think of the other reason why he's so appealing.

Brittney takes a sip of her iced coffee, and the cubes jingle as she speaks. "So you met at a bar, but he doesn't even drink. Your second date was at Madame Tussauds Wax Museum. All sober dates?"

I nod my head. "You know I love my martinis. But let me assure you, David does a dirty very well."

We giggle. "Tell me." Brittney's voice becomes inquisitive, conspiratorial. "You guys have been together since, what, September? Almost four months. What's the most spontaneous thing David's ever done?"

I shrug my shoulders. "He brought me a bouquet of pink roses the other day, just because. It was sweet."

Brittney gasps. "Oh my, flowers! So original. And the worst part is he's kosher! Did you forget that your favorite food is a bacon cheeseburger?"

I cut her off before she can say any more. "Listen, there's a predictability in him that I find attractive. I know what he wants, and he doesn't play games. My life's been so crazy, I'll take stability over excitement any day. Did I mention the sex is great?"

Brittney throws a high five up in the air. "Get it, girl!"

I squeeze her hand, trying to provide some reassurance. "David makes me feel secure. I can count on him."

She stands up, walks two steps over to my side of the table, and gives me a hug. "I get it," she says. "As long as you're happy, so am I."

Days later, my fingers trace the dancing snowflakes that land and stick against the bedroom window. The heat migrating from the hot tea on my lap spreads toward my thighs. I tuck the chenille fabric of the blanket underneath my feet, lifting it toward my knees. I pull at a Kleenex, then turn the box upside down and shake: out of luck. I've been cooped up for forty-eight hours thanks to whichever student gave me this wretched cold.

My phone vibrates. David texts: *Hey baby, come over so I can keep you warm.* I consider his request. Is it worth trekking fifteen blocks in this tundra, with a cold? Then I think of his bed and all of the great things that will happen once I'm in it. He doesn't need to ask twice; I'm out the door in less than five minutes.

The pellets of snow slap my face as I walk. Moisture from my socks begins to seep between my toes and they become numb. My snow boots are heavy, the thick fabric collecting water while puddles grow. I slip and slide through an obstacle course of snow mounds—if only I could catch a cab. I take a wrong step and trip, arms circling to catch my fall. I'm able to grab on to a door handle to my right, and thank goodness it's a diner. The only thing better than cuddling in pajamas with David is a bowl of hot soup. A bell rings as I dart inside, and customers give me dirty looks for letting in the frigid December air. I approach the counter. An elderly gentleman stands next to the cash register, greeting me with a big smile.

My hands brush at the clumps of hail on my jacket. My shivering lips struggle to find the words, "Hi! Can I have an order of matzoh ball soup to go?"

He claps his hands twice. "Coming right up!"

His yell could be heard throughout the entire restaurant, which is embarrassing. I'm standing all alone in pajama pants and clunky semi-weather-resistant shoes. He appears to be in his eighties and has a thick Israeli accent. He speaks with his hands. The curly brown hair on his chest unattractively peeks out through his V-neck sweater.

"Pretty girl like you, you married?" The patrons in the diner stare, also wanting to know the answer.

"No, I'm not. I have a boyfriend, though."

His hands curve up and down in the air as if orchestrating a symphony. "You should have a husband and babies."

How did he also jump on the bandwagon with the Jewish moms of America, needing their children to get married immediately? "You sound like my mother. Did you speak to her before I walked in?"

He hands me the plastic to-go bag, and our fingers graze one another's. I snatch my cold remedy and head toward the door. He says, "Is your mother married? I'd love to meet her." His words become muffled as I pull the heavy door open and offer a polite wave goodbye.

David's building is an old brick structure, the site of the FBI head-quarters in the 1970s. It's fitting, somehow—the lofty ceilings have an eeriness, as if the walls have secrets to reveal. As I enter the lobby, I immediately spot him. A Dartmouth sweatshirt hangs on his slender frame. His curly brown hair frames pale skin, accentuating his pointy nose. His jeans gather in a bunch above his gray Nike sneakers, evidence of his lack of height. He's attractive, in an understated way. He has a fresh box of tissues and a Snickers bar, my favorite snack. He holds the candy out to me. "Whatever it takes to help you feel better." Then his arms wrap tightly around my body.

My cold lips press against his cheek and I dangle the white plastic bag from the diner. "For my throat. I'm already on my way to recovery."

As we enter his tenth-floor apartment, the heat instantly warms and relaxes my body. David throws his keys on the counter and puts his hand on my forehead. "You don't have a temperature. Why don't you just grab what you need from the kitchen and meet me on the couch? I'll turn on a movie."

I rummage through several drawers next to the refrigerator. Where are the utensils in this place? Finally, I grab a silver spoon from the cabinet and a napkin and head into the den.

David has set my bowl of soup on a checkered placemat with a glass of orange juice beside it. His apartment, like many, can't fit a dining table. So I'm roughing it on the couch, leaning over the wooden coffee table to eat. I sip the broth slowly.

But David has anger in his eyes and raises his voice. "Ashley, why are you using that spoon?"

A glob of matzoh ball sits on my lip. "This?" I hold the spoon up. "I need it to eat."

He grabs it from my hand. "Next time, use a plastic one from the to-go bag. You can't use my silverware with food that's not kosher." His nose points down and his mouth frowns like he has just tasted something disgusting. "I thought you'd know better than that, Ashley."

My body freezes, like a small child being punished for doing something that was believed to be okay. In between sniffles, a knot forms in my stomach, replacing my appetite. My head rests against the armrest of the couch and I close my eyes. Now I wish I were at my mom's house instead. She'd bring me tea and toast in bed. I wouldn't have to worry about which spoon to eat with.

At some point that night David must have decided to forgive me because I wake up the next morning wrapped in his arms. I struggle to get out of his strong grip. My cold has gotten worse, and I know where I need to be: in a different bed with a much different person.

Penn Station is quiet this time of day. It's a weekend, and all of the commuters are home in their beds. I can sit on the Long Island Railroad and be at my mom's in less than an hour. Even though I don't live there anymore, it's where I was born and the only house I've ever known.

I stare out the large window of the train as we speed past houses not far from the tracks. Their colors fade together, a canvas of neutrals blurring my vision and focus. The white picket fences and lush backyards evoke of a future that I so crave.

Finally back home, my key turns and before I can push the knob my mom's face peeks out from the other side of the door. "I was waiting for you!" She throws her arms around me.

One would think that she hasn't seen me in weeks, but it's only been five days.

I unbutton my jacket and hand her my hat and gloves. "Hi, Mom! I'm so happy to see you. I feel horrible."

She takes my arm, ushering me down the long hallway to the bedroom. "Ash, now you can relax. I'll take care of you. Come into my bed, it's bigger and you can sprawl out, make yourself comfy."

I hang out in my mom's room all the time, but I never sleep in there. "What about
my room?"

"Don't be silly," she huffs. "You'd really be comfortable in a twin-size bed?"

I consider the option but then come to my senses; she has a point.

My mom's lavish bedroom has changed over the years. Now it's traditional, with a floral carpet, dark brown furniture, and a big plush bed with lots of pillows.

The last time I slept here was in 2001, the day the Towers collapsed. I guess that ever since then I could never get a peaceful sleep there, too much a reminder of what had happened on 9/11 and everything that followed. Of course, the aftermath was just as bad as the beginning.

Back then, my dad loved everything modern. The carpet in my parents' bedroom was black and white, and simple, minimalist furniture graced the space. His little quirks were everywhere, giving life to the otherwise plain space. A blue baseball cap sat on his desk with the insignia of his car; it's what he wore every time he drove. Taped on the wall next to his nightstand were children's drawings. Pastel hearts and rainbows filled the paper, signed by the artist herself: me. Just underneath the artwork was a photo of my brother as a toddler, sitting on my dad's lap in our backyard.

I recalled the clock hitting midnight. It was Wednesday, September 12. I sat on the couch watching the news footage with

Mom. The phone was between us, waiting for a call from Dad, or more likely a hospital. My mom and I held hands in complete silence. We hoped for a miracle, to be proven wrong about what we were guessing to be true. The windows in the house revealed a pitch-black sky, mirroring the darkness of our minds and the unknown. When the grandfather clock pointed to two a.m., and the garage door started to open, we jumped off of the couch and ran. A man's voice was calling out, loud.

"I'm safe! Where is everybody?" The door flew open, and my brother ran inside, his tall athletic build suddenly becoming childlike as he threw himself into Mom's arms. The three of us stood together, unable to let go.

Mom buried her face into Josh's shoulder, crying. "How did you get home?"

"I drove from Bloomington. It took thirteen hours, but I'm here." Josh struggled to bring a small smile to his face, providing my mom with some kind of solace. "I tried calling the house to tell you I was on the road, but no one answered."

Mom lifted her head, gazing back and forth between my brother and me. For the first time in what seemed like forever, I saw a hint of comfort come over her.

"Our phone never rang," she said. "Phone lines were completely tied up today. Too many people across New York were trying to reach loved ones. There was nothing but busy signals."

The three of us stared at each other. The blue eyes of my dad that my brother and I inherited gazed at Mom, reminding her of what was missing, the other pillar that completed this circle.

Together, we walked into my parents' room. Mom turned on the TV; the newscasters were still broadcasting from downtown Manhattan. Then she lay down in the center of the bed as my brother and I rested like bookends next to her. The voice on the TV became lower, fading away as the minutes passed. Our eyes closed and we dozed off, hoping to wake up to a different reality.

Hours later, I felt a hand shaking my shoulder. "Ash, wake up! I can't sleep."

I wiped the sleep from my eyes and saw that Josh was sitting up, wide awake. Mom's breath was heavy and her head was buried under the covers, as if hiding from the cloud of smoke that had been chasing people on the streets at Ground Zero.

Josh rubbed the temples of his head. "I had a nightmare about Cantor Fitzgerald, about the office, and the people."

I squinted as he slowly came into focus. "How did you know the employees?" My voice was raspy, as if the screaming in my head from earlier that day was real.

"Ash, I interned for Dad there, remember? All summer long up until last month. I dreamed of the floors at Cantor burning. I saw the fire and all of the people, oh god, the people!" His hands covered his eyes. "If the attacks happened a few weeks earlier, I would have been in there."

On my mother's bed now, nine years later, I still can't shake the tingling in my bones. The words that had come out of Josh's mouth still give me goosebumps. He got lucky—if we can consider ourselves fortunate at all in this situation. I refuse to let my mind wander into the neighborhood of thinking, *What if we lost Josh that day, too?* I can't go down that road, I won't.

But Mom had wiped the slate clean and redone the bedroom, maybe in an effort to create a fresh start? She even has a boyfriend now. They go out to dinner and movies. He sends her flowers on random occasions. It's nice to see her smile again, in a romantic capacity. After yesterday's kosher conundrum, I'm beginning to wonder if David can accept me for who I am. Or is he only good to me when I fit into the mold of what a perfect Jewish girlfriend should be?

To keep kosher or not to keep kosher, that's not really the question. The images of a husband and children run through my mind—a legacy for my father. I have the hope of a baby boy running around, potentially with my dad's intelligence and blue eyes. David's a step closer to getting there, but if I know anything, it's that tomorrow isn't promised. I've witnessed that firsthand. Life is short. Do I waste my time trying to find the perfect man when I already have a good thing going? These are the moments when I wish my dad were here, to give me his advice in black and white. Then I'd know exactly what to do and which direction to take.

5

Shanghai Garden

It's now April of 2010, and David and I are about to celebrate Passover. We're taking our next big step as a couple, going to each other's parents' homes for the Seder. I've never visited his childhood home. Will he have a Mets or Yankees poster in his bedroom? Will there be souvenirs from family trips and old photos of ex-girlfriends? I muse about all of the little pieces of his history that make him who he is.

David pulls up to his parents' house in Westchester. A circular driveway leads to a quaint, brown-shingled home. A rusty basketball hoop rests beside the garage, evidence of children long gone. Through the small glass windows of the dining room, I can see his mom lighting candles on the dinner table.

I eagerly open my car door and step onto the driveway.

David calls out, "Wait a sec!" He reaches into the back seat and begins fiddling around with a red stick-like contraption. Honestly, I've never seen anybody make this much effort to protect their car.

"That thing looks like a weapon. What are you doing?"

David points to the house next door. "New neighbors. I don't trust anyone. It's a security lock for the steering wheel." He clips it tight.

My teeth begin to grind together. "David, we're in Scarsdale. Who's stealing your '94 Grand Cherokee? Wouldn't the thief be better off with the BMW in the driveway across the street?"

He turns his head, exiting the car.

I climb bluestone steps leading toward lanterns that frame the front door. His mother holds out a bear hug gesture and rushes toward me. "I'm Debbie, David's mom." She steps back; her hands sit on my shoulders, her grin growing wider. "David was right, you are beautiful. Please, come in and I'll show you around."

David's father tilts his frameless eyeglasses downward. "Deb, let's not scare the poor girl." He throws a reassuring smile my way. "Call me Tom, sweetheart, and don't let Debbie's enthusiasm shock you. David's never brought a girlfriend home before, and we're a little excited."

Debbie leads me into each room. David's bedroom has an old baseball uniform displayed on a shelf, along with trophies and signed balls from sporting events. His twin bed reminds me of what I grew up sleeping in, a trundle underneath for sleepovers with friends. Debbie holds my hand as she points to other parts of the house, telling silly stories of David. The time he slid down the banister of the stairs head-first. Or the day he colored the walls of the hallway with his crayons when he was a child. She's kind, and it's clear that she wants me to feel included, like family.

She proudly strides into the kitchen, and I can feel the heat rise as the piping hot oven and stove are hard at work. Debbie stirs a pot with a wooden spoon. "This is where the magic happens!" She laughs at her joke while doing a little shimmy, and I'm drawn to her playful charm.

Then she puts her arm around my back and ushers me toward the countertop. She begins to chop vegetables with intensity and stops, grabbing a knife and holding it out toward me. I hesitate and step away. Debbie laughs. "I see, you're not a cook."

I point to the telephone. "I order in. Trust me, you don't want me anywhere near sharp objects."

Debbie adjusts her eyeglasses and studies me closely. So she's gotten the memo: I'm not the domestic, future wife for her son who will cook every meal and keep a kosher home. But still, she's hopeful, bless her heart. She continues to prepare the food and slowly speaks. "When you get married one day to David, you'll keep a kosher home. It's not easy, especially on holidays like this. Don't worry, honey, I'll show you how it's done." Her voice is cryptic, as if she's going to convert me into some kind of Jewish zombie wife.

I carry a plate of matzoh to the dining room table as Debbie holds a platter of gefilte fish. I sit beside David at the small table for four as we begin the Seder. David hands me a Haggadah and puts his hand on my knee. "These are used to guide us through dinner. It explains the story of Passover."

I hold the book, skimming the pages as if I've seen them a million times. "I know! My family does the same thing."

I mean, we kind of do. Our books are much smaller, the Cliffs-Notes version to be exact. We shortened the Seder down to ten minutes rather than the two hours I knew lay ahead tonight. My stomach growls thinking about how long it would be until I had a piece of brisket in my mouth. Ever so gently, my fingers graze my dinner plate and snap the tiniest piece of matzoh. Then I pop it into my mouth. The stale taste of cardboard has never been so satisfying.

But with just one chew there's a shout from David. "No! We haven't gotten to that part yet!" He takes the matzoh from my hand and places it back on my plate. His family laughs, finding the situation amusing. I stare at the clock and count down the minutes until I can finally eat.

Finally, David and I sit in his car driving back to Manhattan. He flips on the radio and hums a familiar tune. "Ash, what should we do tomorrow night?" He lowers the music and quickly glances over, waiting to hear my response.

I put my hand over his. "Let's keep it simple. Maybe go out to dinner? The West Village could be fun. We haven't been there in a while."

He smirks. "Don't be silly, you know we can't eat out at restaurants during Passover."

I laugh at him; what a silly joke. As he stares at me, his brown eyes squint, and I realize he isn't kidding. "Oh! I'm so sorry, I honestly had no idea that it's an actual rule of Passover."

There's an awkward silence as I try to think of another alternative. "Let's order in, open up a bottle of wine, have a romantic night in the apartment."

He shakes his head. "Ashley, who knows what's in the food we order? It's probably not Passover friendly. Let's just make matzoh pizza."

The next day, our Passover date night, David and I relax in his apartment. We cuddle on his two-seater couch watching ESPN —every woman's favorite. I need to ease the boredom looming over me. I step into the kitchen looking for a snack. As the roar of cheering fans fills the room, I open the refrigerator: nothing good. Time to move on to the cabinets, hoping to find a cookie or bag of chips. Then, out of the corner of my eye I spot a small canister on the counter. There have to be some hidden treasures, maybe some chocolate? I take off the metal lid and put my hand inside. I don't feel anything except some kind of cool metal. I pull it out and come to find the shimmer of a spoon, placed in exile, having been tainted by my un-kosher soup from months ago. David has locked it away in isolation, in this empty jar, the whole time—no longer wanted.

I stomp toward the couch, holding the spoon up to his face. "Clearly, being kosher is very important to you. I respect that, but I'm worried about our lives together. We don't live it the same way."

A frenzy of questions pop into my head, and I begin blurting them out: "What kind of wedding do you want? Do you want a kosher house? Would you want our kids to be kosher?"

David seizes the spoon from my hand and places it on the coffee table. "Ashley, I love you. I'll compromise!"

Compromise sounds like a nice word, but there's always one person who ends up bending. And that person is always me: non-confrontational, always wanting to please. I know I'll end up doing the one thing I don't want to do.

The last big compromise I made was back in high school. It was the one-year anniversary of 9/11, and I had been yelling at my mom, "I don't want to go! I'm not going!" I screamed across the house, and of course she had to be able to hear me. I refused to be ignored.

But then Mom came into my room too calm, too collected. "We're spending the day as a family," she said. She opened my closet, lifted the hangers, looked for an appropriate outfit, and placed it on the door handle.

I grabbed the black sweater she selected and slid it over my head. "Haven't we mourned enough? When does it end?" I didn't know anyone going to this event, and I had zero desire to spend today with them. "I just want to be alone."

I didn't put up a strong enough fight and ended up in the back seat of Mom's car. I was giving her the silent treatment, if only she noticed. My brother sat in the passenger seat, chatting with my mom as if everything were fine. The two of them always had a bond, two peas in a pod—they did everything the same. Both are strong-willed, talkative, and outgoing. I had that with my dad; like a mirror, we saw reflections of ourselves in each other. People always said the two of us were the same: introverted, observant, and at times surprisingly silly. But my counterpart was long gone. So I sulked as we drove toward Manhattan, heading to Central Park, where the ceremony was being held. There would be a huge turnout; all of the victims' families would be there.

A half hour later, I followed my mom and brother out of the car. It was, like 9/11, a beautiful day, sunny and warm. But the wind was unusually intense, as if the souls of the dead were sending messages that they were there. My hair blew wildly across my face, and my mother had to hold her skirt down as we walked. To me, at that age, the only thing worse than attending this event would be the flying up of a skirt to reveal Mom's granny panties.

We crossed Fifth Avenue and headed toward the magnificent boulders and manicured lawns of the park. But an eyesore ahead completely ruined the view. Hundreds of white chairs were lined perfectly together. Many of the seats were already filled. People were dressed in black as if attending a memorial service; maybe we were. My family walked down the center aisle toward the front rows. Howard Lutnick, the CEO of Cantor Fitzgerald, had given us a hug hello. He had dropped his child off at school the morning of the attacks, and that's why he had survived. After losing 658 of 960 employees, Lutnick worked fiercely to keep the company afloat. While doing so, his success skyrocketed, becoming a major name in the business world and among Manhattan's social elite. To be in his company should have been an honor, but I felt nothing but annoyance that a man with such power couldn't give me what I wanted: my father. Lutnick was becoming known at the time for bringing big names to 9/11 events to raise money and awareness—celebrities, musicians, and politicians alike. Indeed, from my seat, I looked up at a large stage to see the singer Carole King, front and center, delivering a speech about 9/11. I didn't hear anything she said, just my own repeating question: why is she here? Then she sang "You've Got A Friend," and the hundreds of faces surrounding me became wrapped in a sea of tears. Yes, the sorrow was tangible, and I felt the pain of every person weighing on my shoulders. But this wasn't what I wanted for this day. I didn't need to think about the buildings or the tremendous number of lives lost. I wanted this day to be about the one life lost that was a void in my heart. This day was about my dad.

I realized at this moment that 9/11 and my father were two very different entities. 9/11 did not define who my dad was. He was special because he was mine, and that's what I wanted to remember on this day. I missed him so much that it physically hurt, and I certainly didn't need a billboard hit to remind me of that.

I was old enough by now to know what was best for myself. This event was right for some people, but I was not one of them. I wanted that to be the last time I compromised on something I knew wasn't best for me.

Back with David, I gaze at him suspiciously, from the corner of my eye.

He begins speaking with authority, convinced he has a solution for our relationship. "Okay, there's just a few things I need in terms of religion to make me happy. First, I need to have a kosher wedding. My grandparents would die otherwise."

I cross my arms, frustrated. "C'mon! Everyone knows that the cocktail hour is the best part of a wedding, and that's because of the sushi and raw bar!"

David takes a deep breath and crosses his arms, too. "I also want a kosher home, this means kosher plates and silverware. If you make a mistake and put the meat on the dairy plate, I'll tell you, and you can fix it."

That's his compromise? A light shade of red sweeps across my face. "If you ever tell me I used the wrong plate in my own home, those plates will be out the freaking window."

He wrings his hands. "Fine, fine, I can be flexible. Don't worry about the china. Just eat on paper plates."

I walk to the other end of the room, unsure whether I'm about to burst into tears or smack him across the face.

David smiles. "I'm so glad we figured this out, what a relief. Oh, one last thing. I know that you love Chinese food, and I can't under any circumstances have that in the refrigerator. So if you order it in then you have to throw the leftovers in the garbage."

I feel the shackles around my ankles vanish. I want to run free, wild and naked, while eating pork fried rice. "I draw the line at throwing away perfectly good sesame shrimp and General Tso's chicken. This relationship won't work."

At that, David begins to sob. I'm not sure if he's crying because of the Chinese food or because I just broke up with him. I pick up my tote, give him a kiss on the cheek, and walk out the door. I know that for the right guy, I'd be willing to bend in any direction, but David isn't for me.

He doesn't try to stop me, either.

The fresh air feels good, and I know I made the right decision. But I'm sad to be single, to have to start dating all over again. Over the honking horns and sirens, I can hear the ring of my cell. The word *Grandma* lights up the screen. She's in her late eighties and the only grandmother I've ever had, because my dad's mom died before I was born. For her, I always answer. "Hi, Grandma! How are you feeling?"

She yells into the phone. "Talk louder, my dear. Your voice sounds sad, what's wrong?"

How does she know? How do mothers and grandmas have that weird sixth sense where they can feel your pain from hundreds of miles away? Or more specifically, in this case, West Palm Beach, Florida.

I break into full confession and tell her everything. Suddenly there's a duet on the other end of the line. "Ashley, you're on speaker. Carl is here, and he wants to talk to you."

Why does my grandma feel the need to put her boyfriend of the month on the phone with me? What could he possibly have to contribute to this conversation?

His heavy Polish accent rumbles in my ear. "Run, Ashley, run!"

I put on a sweet and calming voice. "Hi, Carl, there's no need to panic. I'm perfectly fine."

He clears his throat. "My daughter was in a relationship just like this. He changed her, made her do things she didn't want to do. She's now divorced and miserable. Run, run as fast as you can!"

Carl's extreme concern was kind and somewhat funny. Beyond his antics, though, I agree, he has a point. I reassure Carl and my grandma that I have no plans to get back together with David.

Then my grandma shouts, "Play the field, Ashley, play the field!"

I'm barely five blocks closer to home when my phone rings again. It's my mother—news really travels fast. I pick up, already too emotionally exhausted to have the same conversation again. "I take it Grandma called you."

She sounds relieved. "Ash, I knew from the minute I met David that he wasn't right for you. He shortened your horizons, he held you back. He didn't help you reach your potential."

I thought she'd be angry that I just put myself back on the singles market. "So I wasted a year of my life with someone who you knew wasn't right for me? Why would you let that happen?"

She takes a deep breath, as if I should know better. "You had to figure it out for yourself, my love. That's what life is all about."

I throw my bag down and run to my bed, swan-diving into the pillows. I know that David isn't the guy for me, but I can't stop crying. I feel lost. I'm trying so hard to be a success, and I keep winding up in the same spot I started in, like moving in circles. I grab the picture of my dad on my shelf and stare into his eyes. My tears drip onto the glass frame down to his face. I pretend he's next to me. I concentrate, trying to summon him. I'm desperate to hear his voice again, telling me it will all be okay.

What happens when someone dies? I'd like to believe my dad is watching over me, guiding me somehow. But I don't feel his presence, and I haven't seen any signs. I look around my apartment. An empty bed with no one to share it with. No awards on the wall. No great accomplishment symbolizing that I've done something special with my life. I'm single and alone. A schoolteacher with mediocre success. What else defines me? That I'm the girl who lost her dad on 9/11? Will there ever be anything else?

6

The Devil Wears Nada

Throughout the summer and into the autumn I remain single, with no signs from Dad, of course, and no prospects on the dating front. But the trees are lovely in greens and browns and reds, a reminder of a new season and a clean slate. And the new school year brings a fresh batch of eager students.

Mom calls. "Just checking in," she says, "but where are you off to? It's so loud there."

I press my hand against my other ear, trying to block out the Manhattan street noise, yet sensing there's another reason for her call. "I'm meeting Jill for a manicure at some new salon she's been wanting me to try."

She takes a deep breath. "Would you be able to come home tomorrow? You can spend the weekend, and there are some things

I'd like to discuss about Dad."

Angry New Yorkers bang into me in a hurry as I stop in my tracks. I step under the awning of a building, trying to figure out what to say. I have a hard time talking with Mom about Dad. It's been nine years, but I just can't go there yet. My family usually respects that.

Mom breaks the silence. "I received a phone call a few months ago. The 9/11 memorial museum is moving forward. It's probably going to open next year, and there are some decisions we need to make."

My stomach begins to ache, and the word "museum" lingers in my mind. "Why can't it become a cemetery? That's what it is! A burial ground. Not some tourist attraction for people to visit. This is our lives!"

She responds quickly, upset with my tone. "Trust me, many years from now when you have a family, you'll take them there. It will keep the memory of Daddy alive forever, and it will tell our story."

Through my sobs and sniffles all I can manage to say is, "Sounds really nice."

I know I've hit a sore spot. I inherited the sarcasm gene from my father.

Mom begins to lose her patience. "This is serious. There was a World Trade Center Site Memorial Competition. It was international and a huge deal; architects from around the world submitted ideas."

The bitter lump in my throat begins to rise and I swallow, fighting the urge to vomit. "It's a competition? What is this, a game show?"

She cuts me off, not allowing further argument. "Enough! You will come home tomorrow to help pick out some of Dad's clothes and photos of us as a family. It's being requested—these committees need artifacts, items that belonged to the victims to display in the museum. Josh will be here to help, too."

I don't answer. Mom's the head of the household, and I know not to disrespect her when discussions become this heated. Besides, it's been hard for all of us; I can't imagine how hard for her. She had been with my dad since she was sixteen years old, and they thought they'd be together forever. Now here we are, discussing how to immortalize him behind the glass wall of a museum.

I wipe my eyes with the sleeve of my sweater, black mascara staining the white fabric. "Okay, I'll catch a train in the morning. And Mom? I'm sorry, I hope I didn't hurt your feelings."

Her long pause suggests that I've worn her out, but she'll never admit it. "Don't worry, baby girl. I'll see you tomorrow."

I continue walking, agitated, not just about the conversation but about the way it ended. "Baby girl" was my dad's nickname for me. Hearing it now makes me cringe, but I don't have the heart to tell her to stop.

As I get to the salon, I catch a glimpse of myself in the reflection of the spa window. Jill sits on a black leather bench, waiting. I can only spot the back of her, but the fringed handbag and Grateful Dead T-shirt are a giveaway. I don't want her to see that I've been crying and try to quickly fix my makeup. I'm still anxious, anticipating going home and rummaging through my dad's belongings. How does 9/11 always manage to seep into my daily life? Is there ever a day off from it? But, as usual, I put on a smile and pretend everything is fine.

Jill stands to greet me, and I give her a hug. The empty waiting area is void of tables, chairs, and nail polish fumes. I'm confused. "What kind of place is this? I thought we were getting manicures?"

She pats my thigh with a mischievous smile. "Get with the program, it's 2010! Did you really think I was going to take my single friend out for a boring mani-pedi? You need the latest and greatest."

There's a long narrow hallway leading to a bunch of doors. Suddenly a woman exits one of the rooms with a bashful look on her face. I abruptly stand, finally getting the hint. "Jill, no! You took me to get waxed?"

She laughs and several of the girls in the waiting area stare in our direction. "Not just any waxing, this is a Brazilian." Jill holds up her phone, revealing a picture of her new boyfriend. "He's into it. Once you find your new man, he'll like it too, guaranteed."

I feel reluctant. And terrified. "I've never had any complaints before. What if I end up in the NYU burn unit after this?"

Jill takes my hand and pulls it so that I'm forced back down in my seat. "Thank me for my moral support. It's time to clean up your situation." She waves her hand near my pelvic area. "You're newly single and back in the game, you need a leg up." An overweight woman dressed in a white uniform steps out from the dark hallway. Her voice is baritone with a Russian twist. "Ashley, you ready, girl?"

My pulse rises. I can feel the sweat lingering on my palms. It's like the doctor has just called my name for a checkup and I know a big shot is coming. I walk toward her, looking back at Jill for some kind of reassurance. She's still waiting with a magazine on her lap and yells out: "Get ready for the bald eagle!"

I approach the lady, mortified, as she holds out her hand. "Hello. I am Jackie, and I do your wax today. Come into room, please."

It's a small space with just a table and countertop, doing nothing to help my claustrophobia. I wiggle off my pants and lay down, looking around to find a distraction. On the wall adjacent to my body are pictures of the ladies who work at the salon with their professional certifications. This was very responsible; it's not like they're about to perform open-heart surgery, but good to know I'm in the right hands. I scan the faces in the pictures and find Jackie. Everything on her license seems legitimate. Except that her name is really Svetlana.

Svetlana holds up a stick with wax stuck on the end. "Okay, we begin!" She takes my right leg, throws it behind my head, spreads the wax on my skin, and rips it off. I let out a scream—the hot liquid burns!

As the suffering continues, Svetlana shakes her head in disappointment. "No man is worth it." Then she takes a step back and admires her work. "Beautiful! Now we vajazzle."

I jump off the table and grab my pants, stumbling while trying to put my foot inside.

Jackie takes out a menu and hands it to me. "You see. The vajazzle very nice. Makes man happy."

I read through the smorgasbord of options explained in detail, with pictures included. An array of bedazzled designs sparkle before me. Any option is now at my fingertips, but I hand the laminated menu back to her. "I don't think this is very me. It's so bright and loud. It's too . . . razzle-dazzle for my taste. I'd prefer for my vagina not to look like a disco ball."

Svetlana walks me to the cash register. "You make mistake, lady. The men love vajazzle."

Jill and I reconvene at the front door, newly groomed. She waits for my seal of approval. "Okay! It wasn't so bad. Thanks for pushing me to do this. By the way, did you take them up on their vajazzling services?"

She grabs my hand, concerned—we're two steps out the door. "You didn't vajazzle? Jennifer Love Hewitt was just on *The View* raving about it. It's the thing to do right now."

I'm shocked. But such a fan. "Really? I love her! She's dated so many guys, have they all seen her vajazzle? Carson Daly? Jamie Kennedy? John Asher?"

Jill waves her hand, unenthused. "Don't get too excited, all of those relationships went sour. Maybe Carson went down on her one night and accidentally choked on a Swarovski crystal?"

I laugh and stumble on the pavement. "Someone should really put a warning label on that vajazzling system. Regardless, who wouldn't want to look like Jennifer Love Hewitt? Even if only from the waist down?"

As we continue down the street, my mind wanders again to what's still to come. Not even my silly time with Jill can distract me. I hate facing this part of my past. I try to keep it buried somewhere, hoping that if it stays below the surface, I can manage to continue living a "normal life." In my heart, I know I'll always be a little different. Very few on the planet have lived through the catastrophe that the families of the 9/11 victims have. But I don't want that label. I yearn to be known for something that I do on my own, something positive, something I'm good at. Instead of being connected to a notorious disaster.

The next morning, I arrive at my mom's house and find myself sitting on the floor of my dad's closet. I look up at shelves of clothing, giving the circular tie rack a push as geometric shapes in shades of red dance before my eyes, making me dizzy. A pair of his cowboy boots is beside me; he'd wear them with jeans and a T-shirt on the weekends. It sounds silly, a New York man in clunky leather Western boots, but he pulled it off. He was so handsome, tall and commanding in any room. Whatever he wore he always made look good. I find a pile of baseball shirts, white with colored sleeves. I stand up, going through them, each shirt labeled with a different company that my dad had worked for over the years. It was an on-field resume of sorts. I slip a green Fimat tee over my head and let it hang from my body. I grab the bottom of the shirt with both hands, bring it up to my nose, and inhale deeply, wishing for even a faint scent of him. But it isn't there.

I walk out of the closet and my mom and brother are sitting amongst hundreds of pictures spread across the floor. They silently look at images and toss them to the side, moving on to the next batch. I observe the mess. "Don't submit any photos with me in them. My face is not going in that museum."

My brother looks up. "You can't be serious. One day when you bring your children to the museum, you don't want them to see you? How young you were when this happened to you?"

My back is toward him as I exit the room. "My life isn't here to be on display." That was it, I had made up my mind. I'm not like my mom and brother, never have been. They wear their hearts on their sleeves. They want to share their 9/11 stories. Why? I can't imagine. I know that this is sacred. My feelings are private, and what I experience stays close to my heart. I hold it tight, like the last piece of my dad I have left. Those memories, pictures, and moments will stay with me, locked away and protected.

That night, cramped in the fetal position on my twin bed, the floral walls and pink carpet feel sweet. They remind me of being a small girl and so in love with this room. It was like a secret garden; I was wrapped in the murals of ivy and foliage painted on the walls. It was the perfect place for a child, happy and positive. Still tucked away in my closet were the games I used to play: Mall Madness, Monopoly, and Girl Talk. As I cuddle up under my covers, I remember trying to talk Dad into playing Pretty Pretty Princess. Whether it was his masculinity or knowing it would be sheer boredom, he would never give in.

I recall him coming into my room when he arrived home from work one day. He'd said, "Ash, why don't you wait for me at the front door like you used to?"

I had rolled my eyes with preteen attitude. "Dad, seriously? Wait with the dog at the top of the stairs like a welcome committee?" I was probably on the phone with a boy or doodling in my sketchbook, hoping he would leave so I could continue.

Then he approached my bed, and I stood up on it, making us eye level. I threw my arms around his shoulders, feeling the fabric of his suit jacket while I hugged tight. We smiled at one another, and then he asked, "Please, wait for me next time?"

I never did, but he continued to ask. When my dad died, our dog Taffy waited by the steps every day for a year.

Now I can't sleep and look over at the clock. It's eleven p.m., but the emotional exhaustion from today makes it seem much later. My family have always been night owls, and it's not unusual to find one of us in the kitchen eating a bowl of cereal long after midnight.

I open the door to my mom's room. She's wide awake, at her desk chair. I find a spot on her bed and watch her punch numbers into a calculator. Other women her age might be typing their credit card digits into the computer as they shop online at Saks Fifth Avenue, but not my mom. After Dad died, she took over his responsibilities of paying the bills and overlooking the finances; she left no stone unturned. Her hair is half up, pinned back just above her ears. Her eyeglasses balance on the tip of her nose, and her tailored button-down shirt flows over her fingertips, the white cloth moving with each tap.

I become emotional watching her. This wasn't the job she signed up for, but she took it by the reins. "Mom, you look like a sexy librarian right now."

She continues working. "Very funny, Ash! I'm trying to concentrate."

An overwhelming stack of papers is piled high on her desk, like a moat around the perimeter of her workspace. A checkbook lies next to her calculator, and I wonder if people still use those anymore. A notepad on the other side has a custom heading labeled: FROM THE DESK OF RISE GOLDFLAM. The chestnut desk drawer is open, with documents peeking out.

Beyond the everyday minutia in the drawer are other things, hidden and tucked away in the darkness. Dad's one recovered item from Ground Zero is in the back: a blue credit card, the color mostly burned away. The numbers are almost illegible. The name JEFFREY GOLDFLAM hasn't faded though, and that's all that remains of my dad from that day. The metal of the card was so thick it withstood the sizzling temperature of the fire. Next to the card is a pair of cuff links that my grandfather had given my dad at his bar mitzvah. They were very special to him, and so my mom keeps them nearby. Next to those are my dad's eyeglasses. He had Lasik surgery just weeks before the attacks. Prior to that, he wore his glasses every day. These are our reminders of him, these trinkets now collected beside my mom.

I roll off of the bed and walk over to her. "You should write a book, Mom. All of the people out there who have lost a spouse can learn so much from you."

She doesn't look up from her calculations and continues writing in her checkbook. "Oh, yeah? What would I call it? And what would it be about? A widow's guide to survival?"

I clap my hands. "Yes, in a way. It should explain how you were a housewife whose husband managed the bills and finances, like

so many households do. And once Dad died, you taught yourself everything: the bills, the checkbooks, the college tuition, the
bank statements. You're an inspiration."

"I'll call it *Funding for Fendi*," she says in a joking manner. "Speaking of which, tomorrow, let's go support the economy. It's time to
do some shopping."

She smiles at me, setting aside the bedazzled pink calculator.
Wasn't it just yesterday that I was confronted with the same
sparkly crystals? To be used for an entirely different purpose.

I press my lips together to keep in a small laugh, feeling guilty
that I can have such a preposterous thought after the serious-
ness of our day, picking through my dad's most intimate belongings.

I take her hand to get her attention. "Mom, do you ever feel like
you're expected to choose between being sad and being happy?
And neither place feels exactly right?"

7

A Photo in Black and White

Months pass, and the air grows brisk—it isn't long before Thanksgiving is over. I cuddle underneath the big comforter on my bed, not wanting to leave the warm nook. I relish the luxury of Saturday afternoons, ordering in lunch and doing absolutely nothing. Today, it's my friend Kirsten's birthday. A Christmas baby, she planned a party for herself tonight. Hangers screech as I veto dresses in my closet, the colors and fabrics creating a mural as they drag across the metal rod, pushed aside for something better. My feet step off the cold tile, slipping into a bodycon ensemble. It hugs my waist, and I pull the thin spaghetti straps over my bare shoulders.

That evening at a bar called Fiddlesticks, Christmas jingles fill the air. The lively West Village pub reeks of stale beer, a reminder of college fraternity parties. Single drunks run amok as I feel a hand at my side and turn around, falling into a strong bear hug. Kirsten squeezes me tight. "You came!"

I hand her a fresh cocktail. "Of course, birthday girl. I wouldn't miss it! God, we are getting old. What is this, twenty-six?"

She takes a big swig of her drink and makes a sour face. "Don't remind me!"

I look over the men in the room, all dressed like Santa Claus. Kirsten's green-and-red dress plays a dainty jingle as she moves, little bells hanging from the hem beside her thighs. A furry antler headband sits above her platinum hair.

My fingers flick the bells beneath her skirt. "What exactly is this?"

She waves her hand around the room to showcase the event. "It's Santacon, Ashley. In honor of Christmas, it's everyone's duty to dress up in their most ridiculous holiday costumes and drunkenly parade around. Did you not get the memo?"

I tug at the straps of my dress. "I guess Santa forgot to fill me in, being that I'm Jewish and all."

She laughs. "C'mon, there's a guy I want you to meet."

The floor creaks as peanut shells break into pieces under the soles of my shoes. Kirsten pats the back of a man in a flannel shirt. "Dan, there you are! This is Ashley, my sorority sister from Penn State."

She gives me a wink and shouts, "Play nice!" then struts away.

I shake his hand, struck by his blue eyes and light skin. He's tall, and there's a kindness in his smile, an innocence that tells me to trust him. He holds up his right hand to get the bartender's attention. "What are you drinking?"

I become a bit shy while also trying to ignore the inebriated Santas bumping into me. "I'll have what you're having." He hands me a rum and Coke. He sips his drink, and I can feel his eyes taking me in. We talk for a few minutes, leaning in close to one another, trying to have an actual conversation among the clinks of drinking glasses. His delicate features reflect his youth; he can't be older than twenty-four.

Dan places his hand on my waist, bringing me toward him. "I can barely hear a thing. Want to get out of here?"

I nod and we bolt for the door. I turn around, hoping Kirsten isn't offended that I'm leaving her birthday celebration so soon. But then I catch a glimpse of her in the corner, making out with a guy dressed as Jesus.

Heading downtown, Dan and I walk side by side, shouts from other loud bars interjecting into our conversation every now and then. Our hands brush one another's, fingers grazing like a game of footsie. Approaching Chinatown, the miscellaneous twinkle lights from store windows and awnings allow me to appreciate the silky honey tone of his hair. A street vendor is selling black-and-white snapshots of New York, scenes of Central Park and iconic buildings.

Dan flips through the white mat frames, scanning the images. "How is it that we've never met before? I want to know more about you. What's your family like?" He studies me, and I can feel the chemistry between us.

I try not to mention my dad until I really like a guy. I divert the question as best I can. "Oh, I'm boring, all the usual stuff."

He's quiet, looking through the photos as if trying to find just the right one.

The truth is I'm scared to open up about my past. What if this connection between us is completely in my mind, and I never hear from him again? Why open up if I'm going to get hurt? So I change the subject. "You first, where are you from?"

Dan smiles. "I moved to New York from Poland when I was three. My parents wanted my sister and I to have better opportunities. They both work as chemical engineers upstate, and that's where I grew up."

I'm fascinated. He's unlike the men I usually meet, having grown up in the tri-state area. "So do you speak Polish?"

"*Tak!* That means yes. My parents only speak to me in Polish. It helps when I go back to Europe to visit my grandma and cousins, I can communicate with them better."

The elderly Chinese vendor seems intrigued, listening to our conversation as we look through his photos. Dan politely hands him a five-dollar bill and picks out a picture, handing it to me. "A souvenir from tonight."

I study the photograph, revealing an old Manhattan skyline. Naturally, my eye drifts downtown, provoking a sense of sadness.

Dan and I stop walking and take in the view. The Freedom Tower is framed perfectly between the eastern and western sides of the streets; it's like a painting, bordered by pictograph graffiti and colorful tea shops. We admire its beauty, awed by its tremendous height among the tiny storefronts and small buildings that characterize this part of New York.

I was here a decade ago. I know, because the red and gold lanterns and Chinese writing on the brick walls never age, a constant in this forever-changing city. Butchered geese and ducks hang in the windows, and the smell of fresh egg rolls and lo mein filters over the narrow sidewalks. I stood in this very spot with my family just a year before the attacks.

It was 2000, and I was fifteen years old. My family had just left a casual Chinese food joint before taking a field trip to visit my dad's new office.

He was recently hired to work for Cantor Fitzgerald and was raving about the offices and floor space at the company. He spoke of immense space, professionally decorated conference rooms, and statues fit for a museum. I hadn't been to the World Trade Center since I was a very little girl, maybe seven years old. Now an anxious teenager, I didn't like heights and had issues with elevators due to my claustrophobia—a bad combination when visiting Dad's office on the 101st floor.

I stood in the street, looking up at the Towers from a distance, my dad pointing high in the sky to the antenna. "We're heading there."

A pit formed in my stomach; I didn't want to go there. We walked into an empty lobby, and security asked for my dad's work pass. It was quiet, after dark, and a weekend. Shiny marble hallways led to the elevators. My dad pressed the up button as my mom and brother giggled in excitement.

Dad put his arm around my mom's shoulder. "We take this elevator to the seventy-fifth floor and then a separate, smaller elevator to the 101st floor. We should be up in a few minutes."

I took a step backward; my heart was beating fast. "I can't go up there. I feel sick."

My dad went to my side and held my hand. "There's no reason to be scared. I just want to show you where I work. It'll be fine, just follow me."

My family entered the elevator, and my feet remained planted to the floor. "It doesn't feel right to be up that high. I'm not going to do it."

The elevator doors closed, with them inside. The last thing I saw was my dad's face as he shook his head, upset with my decision. I sat on a small bench in the lobby for a half hour, disappointed in myself for letting him down. But for some reason, even then, I had a bad feeling that something with the building wasn't right.

Reflecting on that memory, I never did see the floors of Cantor Fitzgerald. To this day, I can't decide if I regret that decision or not.

Dan's hand is now against my back. "Ashley, are you okay?"

I'm startled. My throat is dry, and I want to tell Dan what I'm feeling.

He takes his arms and presses my body against his, hugging tight. I take a deep breath and close my eyes, grateful to be brought back to this moment. My nose is against his jacket and I inhale the oaky scent of his cologne. The touch of his hands against my body makes me feel safe and protected.

Dan's fingers caress my cheek, turning my head to face his. He says, "*Czy moge cie pocalowac?*"

The rolls of the letters against his tongue sound like a charming lullaby, drawing me in.

I look into his eyes, searching for translation. "What did you say?"

Dan lowers his head, and his lips barely reach my neck. I can feel his breath against my ear as he whispers, "Can I kiss you?"

Every inch of him moves with purpose, slow and passionate. His body leans on mine. I can feel his fingers tighten on the sides of my waist. My back is against a brick wall, and I let my arms rest around his neck. My fingers glide in and out of his hair. For the first time in a long time, I have the shadow of the buildings over me, yet I feel anything but pain. Rather, I feel hopeful, sexy, and alive.

Several days later I daydream about my kiss with Dan. It was perfect, and I can't wait to see him again.

So why hasn't he called?

Was the incredible chemistry just my imagination? Or is he just a player like so many other guys? He did invite me back to his apartment after our walk to Chinatown, which I politely declined. Was that it? He didn't get lucky and is now moving on to more promising endeavors? I feel my phone vibrate and quickly take a look.

"So when can I see you?"

I'm excited for the briefest moment, but it's not Dan's number. I have no idea who this is.

I type back: *"Who are you?"*

Another vibration, and the mystery is solved.

"It's Sam, Salwa's dad. Sorry it took so long to get in touch, but I was in the Middle East visiting family for a few months with Salwa."

My back sinks into the cushion of the couch. I had totally forgotten about this guy. His daughter wasn't even my student anymore; it was a new school year. I reply: *"If this is the speed at which you respond to your child's education, then we need to work on your parent engagement skills."*

I can see from the dots on the screen that he is responding immediately. *"Please forgive me! I'll make it up to you."*

I pause. Sam disappears for months, and now he expects me to eagerly join him on a date? I'm not buying what he's selling. But then I think of his dark hair, his flirty movements, and his sweet interaction with his daughter. Meeting Dan was wonderful, but I haven't heard from him, and who knows if I will. So, as my grandma says, I decide to play the field and give Sam another shot.

I write back: *"Why not? Let me know where and when."*

"I'll call you this week to catch up. Mark your calendar for Friday at 5 p.m. at The Other Room."

That Friday I wake up peppy and eager to start my day. I need an outfit that can carry me from work to a date with Sam, without changing. Something that shows off my figure but is appropriate enough to wear in front of my colleagues. I grab a pair of beige dress pants from my closet with gold buttons along the waistline. I throw on a black tank and over that a sophisticated blazer. The jacket would be coming off prior to my date. I squeeze my feet into a pair of high black pumps, rolling my eyes. I know I'm going to hate myself by the afternoon; my toes are already pinched.

The school day moves along quickly, but I have butterflies in my stomach anticipating the night ahead. I walk around the classroom, setting up for the next lesson, filling empty jars with paint brushes and laying out construction paper and scissors. The children chitchat while working, productively drawing, cutting, and painting their creations. Then I hear shouting by the sink and see several of the girls acting crazy. They've dipped their hands in neon green paint and are waving them around in the air, threatening to ruin each other's outfits. They each run in various directions, laughing and trying not to get stained.

I dart over before it's too late. "Girls! Stop it, you're going to get the paint—"

Mid-sentence, the students freeze, all trying to hold in giggles. I look in the mirror opposite the sink, turn around, and find a small green handprint on my butt.

"Oh my gosh! Who did this?" The children break out in laughter and, in my embarrassment, I join in. My beautiful ivory pants are now green.

Finally, I dismiss the children for the day and rush out of the bright red doors. I hail a cab downtown and realize the subway would have been more economical. But stained pants or not, I want to arrive at my date looking put together, not like I hiked flights of stairs and transferred three subway lines to get there.

Sam's waiting for me at the street corner outside of the bar. I exit the taxi and walk toward him. He holds out his hand, reaching for my fingers, raising them to his mouth and giving a kiss. "My lady," he says, with a bad interpretation of a British accent.

It feels like only yesterday that I had last seen him. He hasn't changed at all. "Well, it's nice to finally see you again. Should we go inside?"

He holds open the door. I feel the heat from the bar and am immediately warmed. He points to a table in the corner, surrounded by velvet chairs and a fireplace. "I reserved it for us."

I take a seat, getting cozy by the fire. He sits across from me, looking around, as if searching for someone. A good-looking man approaches our table with a big smile. It's about time. I need to order a drink to calm my nerves.

Sam stands, giving our waiter a kiss on the cheek. "Hi, honey!"

I look at Sam, confused. "He isn't the waiter?"

Sam laughs at my joke, although I am nothing but serious. "Ashley, meet Eddy, my boyfriend."

Eddy takes a seat, unbuttoning his jacket and cozying up next to Sam. How could my gaydar have been so off? Since when is "parent-teacher conference" in a flirtatious tone code for "join my boyfriend and I for drinks"? I'm bewildered until Sam breaks the awkward silence. "Ashley, I'm so glad we all finally got together. Eddy's in grad school for his teaching license, and I thought you could give him some pointers. Plus, you were such a great teacher to Salwa, and the least I can do is buy a round as a thank-you."

I need to get out of here. "I'm suddenly not feeling very well," I say. I hope I'm not rude, but I stand up, throwing my coat on quickly. I look at the men to say goodbye, but they're too busy gazing into each other's eyes to notice I'm on my way to the door.

Outside the bar, I peek through the window—Sam's watching me walk away. At least that's what I think he's doing, since apparently he's not checking out my body. Then I realize what it is: he's staring at the painted green handprints on my butt from earlier today, waving goodbye.

I speed walk to the subway, desperate to get out of this area and be home in my bed. As I push past crowds racing to catch rush-hour trains, I bang shoulders with a tall man. I look up—why doesn't he watch where he's going?

It's my brother looking down at me. A big smile graces his lightly bearded face. "What are you doing here?" He takes my arm, guiding me off to the side to avoid being run over by speedy pedestrians. "Let's go for a drink!"

The thoughts of TV and sweatpants have vanished from my mind. "I desperately need one."

We find our way to a local pub, order vodka sodas, and unpeel the layers of winter gear from our bodies. Josh gets a round of shots, too. "I'm assuming you had a bad date?"

I take a sip of my drink. "How can you guess?"

He pushes the shot glass toward me. "Pretty outfit, nowhere near your school or apartment, and walking home alone. Dating is the worst."

I point to his left ring finger, enveloped in a platinum band. "So, marriage, is it everything you thought it would be?"

He twists the ring and stares down at it. "You know Daddy never wore a ring; he said it bothered him when he typed. I totally agree, but Rachel would kill me if I took this thing off. I swear, women hit on me more with it on!"

I take my shot, chasing it with water, not helping with the burn. "Do you think Dad would have agreed? That women want what they can't have? More interested if you've got a ring on your finger?"

He looks at me like I should have been in on the joke. "Daddy's the one that told me that."

A bit of jealousy comes over me, wishing I had those conversations and moments with him. But I was too young, not yet old enough to get to know him as an adult, as friends. He was still very much the authority figure in my life before he died, the loving and supportive father and enforcer of rules. I wonder what advice he would give me now. As an adult father to his adult daughter. Rules are no longer needed, and guidance becomes offered advice, not mandatory requests. But I'll never know.

If my dad were here, would I already be settled with my dream guy? Would my career be in a better place? I feel like I'm letting him down somehow. Yes, I'm living my life, having been through the worst with him being killed. But is this good enough? Am I good enough? Dad was always a success. A Wall Street tycoon, happily married with kids, able to provide, to take care of himself and the people he loved.

I never did feel quite at his level. Never smart enough, needing tutors most of my life, and more of a free spirit, go-with-the-flow mentality. Part of me thinks he must have worried about my future, whether I would be able to handle taking care of myself financially and emotionally. I was such a flighty little girl. And has anything really changed?

I can clearly picture his face when I refused to see his office all those years ago. Weakness takes over my muscles, a sense of illness coming over me. His look of disappointment is piercing through me, now answering every question I've raised.

8

Leaving the Nest

I wiggle under the covers, trying to find a warm spot. I wrap my arms around Dan's body, close my eyes, and think back to more than a year ago, when we first met. It's hard not to laugh about it now. The day after our romantic walk through Chinatown, Dan drunkenly dropped his cell phone in the toilet, which is why he never called. It took him about a week to find my number through mutual friends. I'm grateful for his persistence. I never thought a night at Fiddlesticks could result in finding love. Is this love? I think I've fallen for him.

His chest moves slowly up and down. The morning light hits his hair and perfectly traces his silhouette, curved along the sheets and pillows. I gently get up, heading toward the large post-war window of my apartment. The once thin and bare branches outside have been taken over by small green leaves, a sign that spring is here. I draw the shades and keep out the light.

Hours later, Dan watches as I nervously pack. The floor of my bedroom is covered with sweaters and pants that I ruled out, throwing them on the chevron rug. He lays in my bed as a basketball game plays on the television. There is something sexy about him under my covers, leaning on the pillows, wrapped up in my world. It makes him a part of my life, and I like it. I observe the clutter of clothing surrounding me and need a momentary breather. I reach for my mug, appreciating the hazelnut coffee. I take a bite out of my everything bagel and watch as the seeds fall to the floor, missing the plate. Why not add to the mess at this point?

I turn to him. "Thanks for running out and grabbing breakfast earlier."

Dan manages to separate himself from the game and gives me a smile. "Anytime we wake up together, that's what you'll have. It makes me feel good to take care of you."

My heart jumps. Could he be any sweeter?

He comes to me and starts folding the piles on the floor. "You're just meeting my parents. There's nothing to be nervous about."

As we crawl on hands and knees, attempting to clean up my wardrobe, my face meets his with a kiss. "This is why I love you. You keep me calm during unnecessary meltdowns. Look! I've taken my stress out on my entire closet."

My face is bright red. Did I mean to say "I love you"? It just slipped out of my mouth. Maybe he didn't hear me. I can't believe I said it first.

Dan observes the evidence scattered throughout the room and laughs. "If it were up to me you wouldn't need to pack any clothes at all." His fingers trace my bare back, outlining my black lace bra. He moves the strap down from my shoulder and presses his lips on my skin. "You're most beautiful just like this. By the way, I love you, too. And for the record, I was planning to say it first."

I shove extra sweaters into my weekend bag and try not to lose my cool. I'm internally doing cartwheels, basking in the glory that Dan and I are in love. I try to distract myself, going back to the task at hand. I'm going to be staying at his parents' house for the weekend. I have no idea what they're like except for the stories that Dan's told me. They grew up in Poland when it was still communist-ruled. Their childhoods were tough. They had moments with no food or money, and that mentality was still very much a part of them.

My dad used to tell me stories of his childhood. His father had been in World War II and later went to work in the New York City Garment District. They didn't have much. My father played soccer throughout his childhood, and his black horn-rimmed glasses were always taped together because my grandparents couldn't afford to pay for a new pair with every ball to the face. Still, I imagine this was a far cry from communist oppression.

I sit on my bag as Dan, in a team effort, zips it shut. He throws the duffel toward the front door and holds out his hand to help me off the floor. "You know, I was nervous when I met your mom, too. And it worked out, it always does."

To travel to Saratoga, where he grew up and where his parents live, Dan and I drive for hours past empty barns, soft wooded hills, and rolling landscapes. With every mile away from New York City, the air becomes clearer. I open the window wide, closing my eyes and inhaling the scent of fresh April grass and tilled fields. The farmlands are speckled with cows and fruit trees. Picturesque red barns feature American flags waving in the breeze. I feel free from the sirens and chaos of the city.

I turn toward Dan. He's quiet, no talk of politics or work, as there usually is. He hasn't even discussed plans to see old high school friends while we're in town. Something is different, and I hope he isn't nervous, wondering if his parents will like me. I join in the silence, cranking up the radio as Dave Matthews plays, a reminder of teenage years.

Now off the New York State Thruway, we weave through local streets until the road follows a creek. Water ripples across small rocks against the land. The stream flows past houses, as if guiding us to our final destination. Well-maintained homes sit side by side, all colonial, in shades of beige and white. Each has a porch with Adirondack chairs overlooking manicured lawns with beautiful flowers and plants. It's a quaint and charming place where almost every driveway has a basketball hoop and, it seems, a small dog running around on the lawn.

We turn in to a short driveway bordered with rose bushes. As Dan unloads our bags, I gaze upon weeping willows draped along the roof of the house, with bird feeders hidden in the leaves. We walk to the front door. A wind chime hums as Dan's key turns. Suddenly, two heavy Polish-accented voices shout from the kitchen: "Make yourselves comfortable. Dinner's almost ready!"

The voices are friendly and express a hint of excitement, and my discomfort starts to ease. We take off our coats, and I follow Dan toward the kitchen. The décor looks European and antique, the furniture in dark shades of brown and the lighting dim. The design is minimal—a two-seater sofa graces a den with no television. One small painting hangs above the couch, splashing a little color. A beige rug covers the floor. Every shelf, table, and chair has a purpose. Nothing is displayed to be purely decorative. This is a functional house: an accent table to throw keys upon, a shelf with a few family photos.

His mom Lena and dad Pavel run toward me with big smiles, embracing me in hugs. Dan has an uncanny resemblance to his mom, the same round face and similar sweet tone in the voice. His dad ushers me toward a wooden chair by a table covered with food.

Lena proudly points to the platters. "Dan, I cooked all of your favorite things."

Dan takes my plate and begins serving large portions. "This is pierogi, my favorite. It's like a dumpling with meat inside, try it."

He scoops a mound of potatoes next. "These are made with bacon. It sounds weird, but it's amazing."

He continues filling my plate with varieties of meats and breads —there's not a vegetable in sight. His parents fill me in on what Dan was like as a child and what it was like starting a life in Saratoga. Dan's dad reminds me a lot of my father—a man of few words, an observer. But when he speaks, he's intelligent. Everything he says has importance.

Pavel puts his hand on Dan's shoulder. "Ashley, did Dan ever tell you about the time he was in high school? We wouldn't let him go to a party."

Dan starts laughing and interrupts. "No, Dad! Let me tell it. You make it sound so embarrassing."

Pavel continues, ignoring the request. "Dan decided it would be a good idea to go anyway. So he tried to climb out of his bedroom window. Except he got stuck."

Lena's shoulders rise and fall as she giggles, staring at Dan as though he's a little boy, silly and adorable.

Dan holds his hands up in surrender. "Bottom line is I had to scream until my parents heard, came to my rescue, and pulled me back in the house. To top it off, it was the dead of winter, and I was freezing, hanging halfway outside."

Pavel takes Dan's hand and holds it. "Look how far he's come: investment banker, takes care of himself, has a nice girlfriend. We are proud." He smiles at his son adoringly, and my heart stings a little, missing my own father.

Pavel walks to a cabinet above the sink and pulls out four small shot glasses. I've never seen anything like these; they are beautiful, with elaborate designs and long stems, like miniature wine glasses. He sets them down and removes a bottle of vodka from the fridge. The frost on the handle of liquor mixed with the snowfall outside brings me to shivers.

We are each handed a glass, filled to the brim. Pavel raises his in the air. "To my son, we are so happy to have you home. And we thank you for bringing beautiful Ashley to join us. We hope you will come back and visit more often. *Na zdrowie!*"

We all clink our little beverages together and throw back the vodka, the sharp taste causing me to tremble once again.

I peek out the sliding glass doors next to the dinner table. Overlooking a lush garden and patio, the sky has become dark. After hours of Dan and his parents catching up, I'm relieved to finally see Dan's room and relax until bedtime. I follow him, stumbling down a long hallway. "Your parents sure know how to drink."

He doesn't turn around. "Tell me something I don't know!

Where do you think I get my tolerance from?"

"My mom's done one shot in her entire life and it was at my brother's college graduation. I believe it was a fuzzy navel."

Dan grins and shakes his head. "Not even a real shot! Doesn't count."

The bedroom is straight out of the nineties. White Formica furniture sits beside built-in cabinets and shelves. Basketball trophies line the walls, along with academic certificates of excellence. A poster of U2 is stapled above a small wooden desk, in the company of other bands. An electric guitar rests on a stand beside a full-size bed, and before I know it, I run and jump, pillows falling to the floor when I land. I breathe in, content and exhausted, lying on my stomach, head buried in the plump down comforter. The mattress sinks in as Dan's body lies beside mine.

My face leans in for a kiss and his head jerks to the side. "Are you okay?"

He wipes a tear from his eye. "This has all been so perfect. Every second we've been together. My parents love you; I knew they would. And now, I feel like it's going to end."

My heart stops in its tracks. Is he breaking up with me? Seriously? I came all the way to Saratoga to be dumped?

He takes my hand. "My office transferred me to Boston. I have to move this summer. I found out a few days ago and, just, I've been trying to find the right time to tell you. But it's never the right time."

My chest tightens. I've been so happy, and now he's about to leave. "Why can't you find another job? Try to stay in Manhattan!"

He shakes his head. "Boston's a great opportunity for my career. I'd be an idiot to turn this position down. I mean, I guess I didn't tell you that I went there to visit, just a quick day trip after I found out. I fell in love with the city. It's quaint and the history is incredible. I can see us there, you and me, starting a life together. I love you, Ashley."

Once again, the rug has been pulled from underneath me, and I feel sick. He loves me? Move to Boston? Start a life together? I'm like a computer about to crash—I need time to process. That pit in my stomach, the one I had when I realized that Mr. Kosher wasn't the one for me, has returned. Is this another man thinking he can do whatever he wants, and I'll just follow along? Is there something about me that makes my boyfriends think I'm just along for their ride?

My eyes begin to burn. "I'm not ready for us to be over. And I know long-distance relationships are impossible. I've been there, I've tried."

Dan takes my hands in his. "So come with me! It'll be our adventure."

I rest my head on his shoulder. "I need time to think. I love you, too! And what we have I'm not willing to let go of, but this is a huge decision."

He kisses my forehead. "Of course. Let's enjoy the weekend. Take as much time as you need. Just know that I have plans for us, and if you come with me, I'd be the happiest man in the world."

Several days later, I'm back in Manhattan to meet my family for dinner. But first, squeezing in a happy hour with my friends from high school wouldn't hurt. We meet at Session 73, a bar known for good live music and heavy pours. The weekend brings a big crowd, and I shove my way through the door, hoping one of the girls has snagged a spot to sit.

I see Jill's face at a tall table, surrounded by the other girls. I rush over, giving everyone hugs and kisses hello.

Brittney points to a stool. "Ash, sit, we ordered you a dirty martini. I was just telling everyone about the wedding photographer I booked."

I take a big sip. With most of the girls now engaged, wedding plans and honeymoon itineraries are a common conversation theme. I can barely focus, pretending to pay attention to the chatter as I sit in a fog, in a mental tug-of-war about the proposition from Dan.

Brittney senses my apathetic attitude, and I feel a nudge. "Ash, what's new? How was meeting Dan's parents?" Suddenly all eyes at the table are on me.

Jill chimes in. "Isn't it crazy how he looks like your dad? The business-casual clothes, the same blue eyes and fair skin. They're the same person! But in a completely appropriate, non-Freudian type of way."

Everyone laughs. I hope there's no daddy complex going on—I've got enough on my plate. Although, if I were looking for a guy like my father, would that be such a bad thing?

I nod my head in agreement with Jill. "My family loves him, too. They said my dad and Dan would have been two peas in a pod. Discussing finance and politics together."

Everyone falls silent, never sure how to handle the sensitive topic of my father. So maybe I'll spice things up. "I do have some news. Dan's been offered a job in Boston, and he wants me to go with him."

Drums begin banging loudly, and we all hold our ears for a moment, adjusting to the noise.

Jill, sure she misheard, gives me a wave of permission to continue talking. "Repeat that? I thought you said Boston?"

I nod, not bothering to compete with the punk band near us. "That's right," I shout. "Dan leaves this summer. He wants me to go with him. What do you think?"

Brittney slams her drink on the table. "Well, you can't go! What about your job and your family? They would be devastated! You could never leave them. I'm sick of men thinking they can make decisions and women will just follow along."

Jill waits for her turn to speak. I can sense her eyes on my stressed face. She plays the devil's advocate. "I see what Britt is saying. And I agree with the part about your family. I can't imagine you leaving them after everything you've been through together. On the other hand, I've never seen you this happy, Ash. You and Dan are such a great match. From the minute we all met him, we thought he was perfect for you."

No one asks what I think, but I at least appreciate Jill's attempt to see the other side of things.

I take another sip of my drink. The music is deafening, and we're all practically shouting. "Listen, I don't know what I'm going to do! But it's an offer worth considering! I've lived in New York most of my life. Maybe it's time for something new?"

The stares and awkward silence are evidence enough that the girls are not thrilled with the news. I look down at my watch, hoping for a saved-by-the-bell moment. As it turns out, I've gotten lucky. "I'm sorry. I have to go. I have dinner with my family in ten minutes!"

Now sad, I leave happy hour. I wasn't able to share my thoughts with my friends as I had hoped. Obviously, there's a one-way street in my life, pointing in the only direction offered: New York City. I stroll west toward Orsay, the French restaurant my family chose to meet at. The sky has become black, and drunk post-college groups surround me, hustling to nearby bars. With each step, I cool down from the irritation. Anger has migrated to exhaustion. But sick of wedding talk, flowers, photographers, and dresses, I'm needing a change. I want something more than what I have right now.

I approach the large red doors of the restaurant and take a deep breath. I think of my family, all talking over one another at the dinner table, passing food and pouring wine. This will be a relief, I hope, something to get my mind off of the brutal gathering with my friends.

I give each family member kisses hello; they're already seated. A glass of pinot noir has been poured for me. I take a sip as my mom and brother continue an engrossed conversation. A hand graces the shoulder of my mom, his arm gently resting around the back of her neck. My mom's boyfriend Joe sits next to her, politely listening to talk of finance and bills, but I'm positive he's really sleeping with his eyes open. He has the same broad shoulders as Josh. Similar light-colored eyes to me. At this point it's comical when people see our family together and say how much Josh and I look like "our dad." Rachel, my sister-in-law, looks over the menu. Her silky, caramel hair flows down the chest of her knit sweater. Her long, thin fingers grasp the menu as she contemplates what to get while ignoring everyone entirely; I can't blame her. I take in the dynamic of all the personalities and a sentimental feeling comes over me of how much I love everyone.

Rachel holds her glass in my direction, waiting for a cheers. She looks concerned. "I can tell something's not right. What's going on?"

I shake my head in denial. "Everything's fine. I'm just tired."

She puts her drink down and pushes my shoulder. "I've known you for years. You're a sister to me. Don't lie. Tell me what's up."

I give in. She has a point. Rachel's been nothing but amazing, fitting into our unique situation seamlessly. "I promise to call you after dinner. Not in front of them." I look over at my mom and Josh.

Rachel gets my drift. "Enough said."

I look at her left hand, graced with a beautiful cushion-cut diamond, surrounded by pavé stones. "Rach, how did you know Josh was the one?"

She swirls the liquid in her glass and we watch the burgundy swish around. "He made me feel whole. I didn't have to pretend to be someone else. We just understood each other from the beginning. We were best friends. We always made things easier for each other, compromising to make the other happy."

I consider what she's just said. After my last breakup I swore I'd never compromise for anyone again. But if it's love, and I think this is the real thing, should I think twice? A breeze from the open door grabs my attention, and I see Dan walking toward the table. I was so disgruntled by the situation with my friends that I forgot he was coming. I feel like I'm in a haze that's impossible to escape. Is this an anxiety attack? Dan puts his hand on my shoulder, shy to kiss me in front of everybody. He gives a friendly wave to the rest of the table and takes a seat beside me. He talks with my family, but everyone's words sound muffled.

That is, until I hear Dan announce: "Boston."

I'm startled and flustered, unsure of what led him to mention this to my family. I look at Dan, confused.

He squeezes my thigh under the table and whispers in my ear. "You didn't tell them? How could you not tell them?"

I turn away from him, horrified to see the reactions on the faces of my family as they've just heard the news that Dan is moving. I glance at my mom, convinced she will be bright red in anger. Positive that my brother will be the first to speak, scolding me for not telling everyone sooner.

But instead, my mom and brother have morphed into one individual, looking at Dan and saying something along the lines of: "Sorry to see you go."

In other words, "Don't let the door hit you on the way out." They aren't in the slightest concerned about me leaving, or whether I am sad that Dan is going. They just assume I'll be moving on to the next guy.

I'm enraged. Why does no one care about what I want? My fists tighten and my arms begin to shake, and I can't hold back the words: "I'm thinking of moving to Boston, too. I haven't made a final decision, but it would be a nice change."

For the first time in history, the family table is silent. Dan seems in shock, as if he never thought I'd actually give the move a fair chance. My mom and brother stare down at the white tablecloth, unsure of what kind of mental frame I am in to consider leaving them.

My stomach burns, knowing that I've hurt the people I love. My brother had been in a situation like this before, but his relationship ended, his loyalty and proximity to our family paramount. Now here I am, considering whether to break the three of us apart.

Ever since Dad was killed, my mom, my brother, and I have shared a closeness, one that is impossible for outsiders to understand. The days and months that followed 9/11 were like a horrifying, comatose game of musical chairs. The three of us took turns in shock, unable to eat, sleep, or talk. It was the job of the other two to take care of that person and pull them out of their misery. This was when I learned to cook. I still can't, but it was the first time I turned on the stove. It's when I did my first load of laundry. It's when I became an adult. Not only because I lost my dad, but because I had to learn to do things for myself. No one else could.

A few days after the attacks, a survivor list came out. It held the names of people in the buildings who had been hospitalized, so severely injured that they couldn't call family.

We stood in the den of our house as my mom's shaky finger scrolled down the list. Then she yelled out to my brother and me, "'Jeffrey Goldflam'! His name is here, he's okay!" Alongside me, she fell to her knees, as a churchgoer would at an altar. It was the first time I'd ever seen my mom lose her balance, collapse to the ground, and cry into her hands. Sobbing and convulsing, in disbelief that my dad could still be alive.

I, too, was in shock. I didn't help her up or give her a hug. I remained planted, feet stuck like concrete to that spot. I felt numb, like this news was meaningless. That's because I knew it was; it couldn't be real.

Minutes later, my brother hung up the telephone. "I just spoke with the hospital. That list was never professionally verified. People are putting up false names. It's a lie, a complete fucking scam." He sat down next to my mom, and we all cried.

That night, my brother and I together tucked Mom into bed, her eyes still bright red from the tears. My brother fell asleep next to her, and I could do nothing but roam the house, taking in everything familiar. The rest of the world now seemed so unknown to me. When I last peeked into my mom's room that evening, my brother was next to her on his back. Underneath his palm was a four-by-six photo of my dad and him. As he slept, he held it tightly against his chest. I watched the picture move up and down as he breathed.

When I think back on those times, when the moments were tough, the three of us were there for each other. The dings of silverware against plates remind me of where I am, but I can't shake this feeling from all those years ago. Am I really going to abandon them? After everything we've been through? I'd have to be the most selfish person on Earth.

9

Polonia

O f all the places to go for a romantic trip, I never expected that Dan would think of Poland. After all, Warsaw isn't Paris. The white noise of the airplane engine has passengers at ease—asleep or watching movies on the small screens in front of them. And here I am, on a summer break from work in 2012, and I'm the only one fidgeting in my seat. I let go of Dan's hand, rubbing my palms against my jeans. Sweat leaves a slight dampness against my thighs.

Dan's thumb rubs my cheek. "We land in two hours. You've got this. There's no need to be nervous flying. It's the safest way to travel."

I can't look away from the Flight Guide on my mini screen, trying to distract myself from thinking about the thirty thousand feet separating my feet from the ground. "I don't believe that statistic. I've scanned every person on the flight twice, judging to see if they are a terrorist."

Dan gives a reassuring smile. "Before you know it, you'll be eating homemade kielbasa and chatting with my grandma."

I smirk at Dan. "I thought your *babcia* didn't speak English. And isn't she one hundred years old?"

"Actually she's ninety-five and still smokes a pack a day. I'm going to translate for you two, it's all good."

Eventually the loudspeaker interrupts, and a muffled voice talks throughout the cabin. It's the pilot, but I can't understand what he's saying. Something's definitely wrong with the plane. Scenarios begin playing in my mind: a faulty engine, an emergency landing.

Dan translates, "He said we've begun our descent. Anyway, have you given more thought about moving to Boston?"

I'm instantly distracted from my fear of flying, the bigger problem now out in the open. I look into his big blue eyes and can read them like a book, hoping for my answer to be yes.

"It's only June. I know I have to make a decision before the school year starts. I could never meet a classroom full of children and then leave them. So I'm still letting the idea marinate, as they say."

Dan takes out his cell phone, showing me the calendar. "News flash, you'll be starting work in September. That's just three months away."

I put my finger up to his lips, not wanting to hear any more. "I'll come to a decision. Just be patient."

A safe landing and an hour of Polish customs later, Dan drives the rental car. He concentrates on the road, not exactly sure which direction we're heading. Cars speed by, some honking and giving us the finger.

I nudge Dan. "Move it along, grandpa."

His eyes remain on the road. "It's a three-hour drive to Kielza, get comfortable."

As we drive past the industrial edges of Warsaw, mid-size office buildings and stores line the roads. The highway is bustling with morning commuters. Everything appears so normal. What was I expecting? Some kind of city in rubble, I guess. From all of the post-war stories Dan's told me about this place, I imagined the country still in shambles. But Warsaw is ordinary-looking, like a small city that could be anywhere in the U.S., except for the street signs and store awnings and parks and shrines to the Virgin Mary, all boasting words I can't understand.

I turn on the radio and Maroon 5 is playing. I laugh and look over at Dan. "American music! Who knew?" A piece of home is here with me.

But the longer the drive, the more desolate the surroundings become. The corporate offices and stores of the city are gone. Tall grass stretches along empty lands, more barren than the view I had on the drive to Saratoga. Every few miles there's a rundown wooden fence beside a modest house, a simple structure built with brown shingles. No driveways or neighborhoods lead to the door. Just a little cottage here and there, in the middle of nowhere. It seems a bit sad, void of any life or energy.

"Is this what Kielza is like?"

Dan shakes his head. "Not like this. It's barren, for sure, but there are the basics. Small apartment complexes, a local grocery and liquor store."

"Well, if it's anything like what I'm seeing now, then I bet the residents are thankful for those markets. They must be in desperate need of alcohol and cigarettes."

Dan nods his head. "There's still a post-communist feel here. Strangers don't always say hello or wave. Others walk with their heads down. People want to blend in."

We turn onto a small winding street with all of the features Dan mentioned earlier. A convenience store here, a market there. The buildings are very old, with brown paint peeling and becoming rusty. Roads are unpaved, and our bodies jiggle as we drive over rocks and pebbles. There's an eeriness, like the town was built in a different time, never evolving with the rest of the world.

Dan parks in a small lot adjacent to a four-story building. The gray concrete walls frame tiny square glass windows, the shades in the apartments all drawn. We enter the building, and I look around the dark portico. The only light is from the open door; the walls and floors are both dark brown. I look to Dan for guidance. "Where's the elevator?"

He laughs. "Wishful thinking." Then he turns his head and begins wheeling both of our suitcases toward a winding stairwell. "This is the only way up. Didn't you say you wanted to exercise while you were here? Ask and you shall receive."

I begin running up the steps as Dan struggles behind me, dragging our rolling luggage with both hands.

Then he yells, and his echoes bounce off the walls throughout the open hallways. "Don't offer to help. I'm good over here!"

His sarcasm is cute, and I know that even if I offered, he would never let me carry my thirty-pound bag up the flights; he's a true gentleman.

Dan stops on a landing to take a breather. "Top floor, babe. I'll meet you there."

I wait in the corridor and expect a neighbor or two to pop out, but there's no sign of any residents. The wooden floors, scuffed and worn, lead to more yellowed walls that are beginning to peel.

An old lady opens her door, looking from side to side, questioning the noise. Her hair is gray and short, gracing a tan, wrinkled face and thin body. Our blue eyes meet, and she smiles, pointing a frail finger in my direction.

Dan runs past me and into her arms. *"Babcia!"*

Her small hands hold his broad shoulders, and she presses her nose up to his, whispering what sounds like a foreign lullaby.

Dan turns, holding his arm out toward me, and speaks to his grandmother in what I assume is an introduction. I walk toward them and give Babcia a hug. *"Milo cie poznac."* I hope my New York accent hasn't ruined the phrase.

Babcia pinches my cheeks, speaking non-stop in a sweet tone. Even though I don't know the language, her expression and the warm sound of her voice tell me everything I need to know. She's been waiting for our arrival.

We step into the apartment and find ourselves in the den. There's a small green sofa on a red floral rug. A tiny window provides a bit of light. The corner of the room has a kitchenette of sorts. There's a mini refrigerator with a cabinet above. A sink full of dishes sits along a wall leading to a bedroom. I peek in, finding a twin bed with a knit blanket in an otherwise empty room. A small dresser is adjacent to the door.

My claustrophobia kicks in after seeing the cramped space, the dark walls. I need a moment to collect myself. "Where's the bath-room?"

Dan points directly behind us to a doorway, which I had thought was a closet. I sit down on the toilet and the light above my head flickers, the room coming in and out of focus. A clothesline hangs several feet above the bathtub, pins holding underwear and shirts as they dry. As I wash my hands, I try to imagine how three adults are going to spend a week in this place. It's going to be tight.

After I slip back out, Dan notices the worried look on my face and stands by my side, kissing my lips. "Don't worry," he says. "It's a lot to take in. I think this place was built before the war in the 1940s. But we'll barely be here. It's just to sleep."

I give him a skeptical stare. "Where are we sleeping?"

He points to the couch. "It's a pullout."

That night, after seven courses of soups, fish, and meat dishes, I am officially in a food coma. I plop down on the couch and un-button my jeans. "How am I going to eat like this for seven days?"

Dan picks up his shirt, patting his belly.

I shake my head. "I don't feel bad for you, there's still a six-pack there. What time is it? I'm exhausted."

Dan looks at his cell. "About ten p.m. I told my grandma we

would go to the cemetery with her tomorrow; it's where my grandpa is buried."

I object. "That's so depressing. On our first official day here? I hate to be a downer, but aren't we on vacation?"

Dan tries to calm me. "It's not what you think. Polish cemeteries are different than American ones. They're beautiful, peaceful even."

He can't be serious. "How are endless rows of headstones supposed to make me feel relaxed?"

We lay back on the makeshift bed and Dan takes the ends of my hair, twirling the strands between his fingers. "I love when you question things. How strong you are. But learn to trust. This is something you should see."

With that, I let Dan kiss me. Our bodies shift closer together. Our hands explore one another's bodies, and the creaks of the couch follow our movements. I pull back. "Not here!" I whisper. "Your grandma is like thirty feet away."

Dan huffs and continues on. I shiver, feeling torn between respecting his grandmother's home and also wanting to give in to temptation.

Dan throws his body on top of mine, and the sound of rusty metal bangs together, bringing us to laughter. He whispers, "Don't move a muscle, this thing is going to collapse." We try to hold our giggles in, not wanting to wake Babcia. Dan gently rolls off of me. He takes my hand, kisses my palm, and we close our eyes, finally falling asleep.

I wake, rubbing my eyes as the morning sun shines through the little window next to the mattress. No one else is here. I take the opportunity for privacy to dress for the day. But I barely slip a blouse over my head when Dan opens the door, talking with his grandma and holding a tray of coffee and a brown paper bag. The smell of eggs and fresh bread flows through the room, and I'm instantly ravenous.

A heavy breakfast is followed by a short car ride to the cemetery. I hope this part of the trip goes fast.

Dan pulls up to a flower shop and parks the car. "Ash, come inside with me?"

We walk toward the storefront and he takes my left hand, squeezing tight. "Have I told you how happy I am that you're here? Are you comfortable? Is my grandma's apartment okay? I know it's not ideal for our time away together, but it's special to me. Having us all under the same roof. Who knows how much longer I'll have Babcia around?"

I stop walking and give him a long kiss of reassurance. "The living situation is tight. But it's also been fun, an adventure."

He gently taps my butt. "I'll make up for last night. You can be sure of it."

I laugh and run a few steps away. "Babe! Your grandma's watching!"

In the car, I hold a bouquet of blue and purple hydrangeas ornamented with white carnations. I admire the beauty, wishing I could take them home rather than leave them on a plot to rot away, no one to appreciate the vibrant petals.

Upon entering the cemetery, we're greeted by what appears to be an endless garden. Every shade of the rainbow catches my eye. The land is covered with lush flowers and green leaves. I'm drawn forward, the exquisite colors calling my name, and before I know it, I'm walking the paths, my fingers brushing the plants and bouquets. Flickers of light appear like fireflies between the vines and blossoms. Manicured flower beds outline headstones, many with candles in glass vases beside the structures. There must be hundreds of flames, weaving in between the memorial plaques and creating a mystical energy.

Dan puts a hand on my hip, and I'm startled. "Not what you thought, right?"

It takes a moment for me to turn to him, my body entranced. It's as if I'm in an impressionist painting, brushstrokes of objects in deep, colorful oils overwhelming my sight. "It's incredible. How can a place that's supposed to be so sad be this alluring?"

He walks toward a plot, pointing to the last name. "My grandfather. It's a Catholic cemetery. Traditional for Polish standards."

A hint of sarcasm appears in my voice. "So only the Jewish cemeteries are depressing?"

We stand still. Dan places the flowers we bought next to the headstone. I think of my father and am strangely relieved that he's not in a cemetery. My mom and brother feel differently. My mother had a tombstone made with my dad's name. It's placed in a spot with the rest of my relatives who have passed away, a spot reserved for family. I've never seen it. My aunt, uncle, and cousins joined my mom and brother for the unveiling. I stayed at home, hiding under the covers. As far as I was concerned, my dad wasn't there. Not his soul, or his body. It was just a piece of stone with his name, nothing more. To stand around it, crying and depressed, was the last thing I'd ever want to do.

Babcia finds us and begins gesticulating and talking quickly, pointing toward a hill in the distance.

"What is she saying?"

Dan stares at her, trying to decipher the words, her Polish much quicker than his. "She said there's something we should see. She thinks it will be important to you. She says to follow her."

We look at each other, confused. Beginning to walk, I can spot a huge sculpture in the distance. As we get closer, I can see it's made of dark black metal and stands fifty feet in the air. My steps, at first brisk, have slowed down. The statue comes into focus, and I think I know what I'm looking at. I find myself standing in front of two black pillars. My chest feels tight. These are buildings, and suddenly everything becomes clear. I put my hands on the hot metal as the sun shines down. Looking up, I block the rays from my eyes and can see the fault line. A gash separates the structure; just a tiny piece at the edge keeps the building connected. An airplane made of concrete pierces the gap, creating an illusion that the structure is no longer intact. My eyes close, desperately trying to smother the tears. This is Tower 1, representing a moment in time before it was ripped in half, an impending collapse.

The pounding of Dan's sneakers on the grass becomes stronger and he suddenly has me in his grasp as I cry. My head is against his neck and his hands hold my head in place, stroking my hair, trying to make it okay.

"I'm so sorry!" he says. "I had no idea this was here." He turns my body away and coaxes me to walk in the opposite direction. His voice becomes soft and nurturing, and for now I only want to hear that.

"Just keep walking," he says. "One foot in front of the other. Let's get out of here."

Dan whispers to his grandma, and I look up to see her hand on her heart, tears in her eyes. He speaks softly, close to my ear. "I had told my grandma about your dad. How strong your family is. She thought you'd want to see this. She said it's a tribute to your father, to show that the world mourns with you. I know it's not something you want to see; I can't tell you how sorry we are."

How did 9/11 follow me all the way to a small town in Poland? Should I be happy that here, across the globe, the Towers and my dad are remembered? Or should I be angry, frustrated that I can't find relief anywhere? I long for a moment to forget, to wash away the horror that follows me each day, reminding me of who I lost, and worst of all, how I lost him.

That night Dan and I sit on the pullout bed with a glass of wine. His hand gently squeezes my knee, bringing my attention his way. "You okay? It was a long day."

I hold up my glass. "This helps. How am I supposed to share 9/11 with the whole world? People have no idea what it's like to lose a parent that way. I don't care how many tributes are built. It doesn't provide any comfort."

I shiver, the open window bringing in a draft of cool evening air. Dan throws a knit blanket over my knees. "You're right, and I know at home it's even harder. It's in your face all the time. Maybe a change of pace would help?"

I smirk. "You think 9/11 won't find me in Boston?"

Dan shakes his head. "That's not what I'm saying. What I mean is, it can't help living day after day in a city where your dad was killed so publicly. You're always downtown, I know it's hard for you. Plus, you've got your family, and they're great, but they're also a responsibility. Sometimes I think you worry so much about them that you aren't actually taking care of yourself."

I consider what he's said. I don't always do what's best for myself, often putting family first. But I'll never admit it.

Dan puts his hands on my shoulders. "Boston's not forever, it's a pit stop. A place to escape New York for a year or two, get a breather from the place. It might be good for you to live in a new city for a while. You won't have your family, or your friends. But that means you can do what you want. Remember you? That person you always put last."

"I thought you wanted to be in Boston long term? Start a life there, as you said."

Dan takes my hand and holds it tight in his. "I know New York is your home, and I love it there, too. That can be our endgame. To live our life together surrounded by the people you love. So knowing that, want to take a little adventure with me? Slight warning, it'll be a little colder. Rooting for the Yankees may be a problem. And listening to those hardcore accents may be the cause of a major headache. But we will have each other."

We kiss for what seems like forever. Our bodies, sitting upright, slide down to the mattress and we pull the covers high over our heads. Life is unpredictable, but I know that when I'm falling hard, I'll be in his arms when I land.

I've made my decision.

10

Hurricanes and Horas

I can still hear Mom's aggravated voice from a few weeks earlier: "I'm not happy you're moving, and don't expect me to help you get there, either."

I sit upon piles of clothes on the floor, a trail leading to the large black suitcase in the front of my new bedroom in Boston. I fold slowly, trying to get my mother's lament out of my head. My arms still get goosebumps when I think of the disappointment she expressed. I examine the mess of boxes and belongings yet to be organized, shaking as I try to settle my nerves. Have I made the greatest decision or biggest mistake of my life?

Just twenty feet away is the small hallway and winding stairwell connecting the three floors of this old walk-up building in the city's North End. The stomps of neighbors as they come and go have become white noise, muffling my thoughts. The front door flies open and the doorknob bangs loudly against the white wall.

Is it five p.m. already? I've been at these boxes for hours and barely made a dent.

Dan's shoes clap against the espresso-colored floor. I jump up to meet him halfway, running into his arms and wrapping my legs around his body. His fingers squeeze my waist, holding tight. I can feel his crisp white shirt against my skin. I lightly tug at his red necktie, pulling it close as we kiss.

Our noses touch as Dan speaks. "Have I told you how amazing it is to have this kind of greeting at the end of a workday?"

I giggle. "Every day since I've been here. What is it, two weeks now?"

Dan takes a few steps and throws me down on the plush king-size bed in the center of the room.

I land on something hard and wooden. "Ow! What is this?"

He turns my body and begins to dig. "Well, let's see. If we can get through the mounds of clothes here, I think I'll find it."

He pulls out a white wooden jewelry box with pink flowers painted on the outside. He delicately pulls the antique handle open and touches the suede lilac lining of the empty compartment. "I'll fill this one day soon. What does Beyoncé say? I'll put a ring on it."

I cover my eyes, embarrassed on his behalf. Then I run my hands through his soft hair. "Babe, do me a favor: stick to finance."

The following morning, I feel Dan's fingers caress the bare skin of my back. His shuffling around the bedroom is a sign he's heading to work, but I refuse to wake, rolling over and tossing the covers over my head. I will myself to stay in bed, be lazy, and enjoy the morning. But after several minutes I toss the covers and sit up. I need to find a job.

Out of the house and down the cobblestone roads and narrow streets, I sense an old-world charm, almost as if I'm somewhere in Europe. A green sign above my head reads "Hanover Street." Bakeries and intimate espresso bars line the block. Pubs play footage of soccer games as heavy men with tan, leathered skin yell at the screens. Pastry shops are sprinkled here and there, and kitchen vents leak a white powder into the air. The sugar fills the sky, and I swear I can taste it. Little old ladies push past me, as if I'm not on the sidewalk. They speak in heavy Italian accents and have silver chains with crosses dangling from their wrinkled necks. I pass restaurants with names like Panza and Mamma Maria. If I get close enough, I can smell the garlic from inside. Bells are ringing, a reminder that it's noon.

Across the street is a beautiful white church, parallel to a three-story brick building called The Trinity School. The children's artwork in the windows tells me I've found what I'm looking for. It's the first stop of many on the list of schools I plan to visit, picked by convenience in location to my apartment. It's not ideal, a private school and religious institution. But I'm in a new city and need a paycheck fast.

I walk through the large entrance, and it's noticeably different from any school I've ever been in. The marble floors hold statuesque columns of Mary and Jesus. A five-foot cross hangs from the ceiling, and I suddenly have a vivid image of the floors buckling, as if the sacred space senses an outsider has invaded.

A slender woman in her mid-fifties approaches. Pushing the glasses on her nose closer to her eyes, she observes my appearance. Her short gray hair gives the impression of a no-nonsense administrator, but there's a softness in her smile, bringing a kind and welcoming energy. "Hello, I'm Nancy Halloway, the principal. How can I help you?"

I hold out my hand and introduce myself. "I'm a teacher and live in the neighborhood. I'm currently job hunting and would like to see if there are any openings here?"

Nancy stares at me for a good minute, and I'm not quite sure what she's thinking. She nods her head in the direction of her office. "Follow me."

She takes a seat behind a large desk and folds her hands across a pile of paperwork. "So what brings you here?"

It's a Catholic school in an old Italian neighborhood—I need to be strategic. "Well, I moved to Boston to be with my fiancé. We're engaged and soon to be married. I live right down the street and would love the opportunity to be part of the community as a resident and give back in a professional capacity."

I'm mentally pinching myself as the lie easily slips out of my mouth. But there's no way Nancy wants to hear that I'm living in sin with my boyfriend!

I hand her my resume, and she purses her lips, sitting back as she reads. I begin to get anxious. My name and contact information flash in large bold letters at the top of the paper. It's a huge give-away—Goldflam. I'm not Catholic! I'm the furthest thing from it. There's no way she'll hire me. I look down, already feeling defeated.

Nancy places the paper on her desk and proceeds with a series of questions—hypothetical classroom scenarios. As I answer, I know I'm saying all the right things, but I feel like a robot. I'm caught in a trance, an out-of-body experience. Perhaps I'm over-whelmed by the stained-glass windows and statues of saints?

It's foreign here, like I don't belong. And there's that familiar feeling, my stomach rumbling in a nervous rant. This has hap-pened before. Like when people tell me that *their* dad has passed away, *too*. Or when people say they knew *someone* who was killed on 9/11. It's not the same thing. None of those dads were killed the way that my dad was. The acquaintances and links that people have to the terrorist attacks aren't the same as watching your father's office burst into flames, then collapsing a thousand feet to the ground. The man who held my hand when I was a scared little girl, the man who kissed my cheeks and told me no one would ever love me the way that he does—he's what I saw fall to the ground that day. Not the concrete, not the buildings, just him. In a sense, this makes me an outsider, regardless of the situation. Who else has been in these shoes? Who else can hug me and say the exact same thing has happened to them? And as Nancy continues to talk, I wonder if there will ever come a time in my life when I feel I've found my spot, like I'm in exactly the right place.

Time moves forward and Nancy has yet to mention my last name. As she discusses the curriculum, which includes religious instruction, it dawns on me that she believes I'm Catholic. Does she not know the Jewish last name rule? If there's a color, the person is Jewish. For example, green, gold, or silver. Hence, so many Jews have the usual Greenberg, Goldstein, or Silverman. Also, any combination of the three: Greenman, Silverstein, Goldberg.

She stands up, reaching a hand out for me to shake. "Ashley, you've got the job."

I'm shocked—how did this happen so fast? Nancy must see the bewilderment on my face, as she answers the question before it comes out of my mouth. "Listen," she says, "one of my teachers decided to move last-minute, and I've been racking my brain looking for a replacement. Timing, my dear, is everything."

Unable to control my excitement, I hug her. Nancy laughs, amused at my happiness. "Your résumé looks great; I trust you know what you're doing. You can learn the ropes as you go."

In September 2012, I stand at the front of my classroom, rows of desks straight as arrows lined before me. I have done what I could with the space, given the time constraints. Originally a sterile white room with just a chalkboard and a large statue of Jesus hanging above, the space is now transformed. The bright greens and yellows of backing paper along the walls complement science, math, and reading centers. A treasure chest full of prizes sits at the top of a bookshelf in a cozy corner where bean-bag chairs rest.

Over the next few months, I experience a few small bumps along the way. Like the time everyone kneeled at mass, their knees bent to the ground as I stood, aloof. Or the moment when my student pointed to a picturesque exhibition of a baby Jesus with his mother Mary, surrounded by animals and shepherds. The child asked, "What is this?" Luckily my iPhone came to the rescue; ahh, the Nativity scene.

One late October day, the students take turns reading aloud from their religious textbooks. Someone calls out, "Ms. Goldflam, what's the Immaculate Conception?"

I turn toward Greg, my pupil, his red hair highlighting the freckles across his porcelain skin. His childlike, blue-framed eyeglasses suggest he's younger than the ten-year-old he is. My fingers skim the textbook on my lap, hoping to find clarity, some sort of explanation. I press my lips together to keep from giggling.

I stare down at the text filled with answers. Yes, I know what the Immaculate Conception is, but I'm not quite sure how to describe this to a child. Teaching fifth grade, all subjects, I'm a pro. But for thirty minutes each school day my expertise goes out the window as I do religious instruction.

I'm saved from Greg's question when Principal Halloway's voice comes over the loudspeaker. The shriek of the static brings our hands to our ears. "Attention, staff and students, there will be early dismissal today due to hazardous weather from Hurricane Sandy. Parents have already been notified. Be safe and have a nice day."

The children burst into cheers, high-fiving and throwing raised fists in the air as if the Red Sox had just won the World Series. Rain bangs loudly against the large glass windows, and I can see flooding in the streets. The epicenter of Sandy is nowhere near Boston, but even the side effects appear to be dangerous.

At home, Dan and I cuddle on the couch, watching coverage of the hurricane on TV. I feel guilty being here, safe and comfortable. I tuck my body close to his. His warmth is soothing. It's dark in the den, the only illumination from moonlight outside. The television screen captures citizens in distress from the storm. There's an eeriness in the room, perhaps all throughout, like there's a demon in the air, circling our bodies. I'm uncomfortable, exposed and unprotected from the uncertainties of the world and the danger that can strike at any moment.

Dan's fingers wiggle between mine. He kisses my cheek and I feel his breath against my face. "Look at that!" he points to the endless line of cars on the TV, lining the highway, bumper to bumper. "They aren't even moving. Everyone's trying to get out of Manhattan. New York's getting it bad."

I suddenly remember its Jill's wedding this weekend—our first opportunity to go back to New York. "Dan, we have to leave for the rehearsal dinner tomorrow. Is it safe to be on the road?"

The two of us turn our heads back toward the news; honking ensues, and angry drivers shout out their windows.

Dan holds up his hands with uncertainty on his face. "We'll give it our best shot."

The next morning, we drive to my mom's house on Long Island. We manage to get from Boston to New York in record time, seeing as every car we pass is going in the opposite direction, away from the hurricane. Planning to get ready there, the wedding venue is just ten minutes away. Dan and I wait as the garage doors open. Again, Dad's bright red Porsche grabs my heart as it comes into view. Eleven years later, I still can't process it all. I try not to dwell on how much I miss seeing him drive around with a smile on his face like a little kid. If I think too much about it, I'll cry. Dan and I walk past the doors, and I let my fingers glide along its smooth exterior.

Mom sits at the kitchen table, her face buried in her hands. I run over, consoling her. "Are you okay? The house looks a mess, what happened here?"

She whimpers. Her tears mixed with black mascara have hardened and dried across her high cheekbones. "The hurricane, it destroyed the house." Dan stands still in the entryway, taking in the situation.

I wrap my arms around her shoulders, her wellbeing my ultimate concern. "Mom, why didn't you tell me this over the phone? How long has the house been like this?"

Her eyes dart toward the ceiling, surveying the damage. "The trees came through the roof yesterday. I've made a million calls for someone to come and tarp it, to try and make it a little more manageable, but no one's available. Hospitals are ruined, houses are demolished, ripped right down to the studs. This isn't a priority right now. All I can do is wait."

I sprint down the narrow hall toward the bedrooms but stop in my tracks when I see the tree trunks protruding, wild and intertwined like a jungle, planted in the middle of suburbia. This can't be real. There might as well be monkeys swinging from the branches.

I gasp. "How many trees went through the roof?"

I turn toward my mom as she shakes her head. "Not worth counting."

I step into the office, which is now mostly unused. A laptop sits closed on a speckled black-and-white desk, drawers tightly closed with paper clips, staples, and envelopes inside. As a little girl I used to sit on the beige carpet by my dad's feet as he typed. I'd use the office supplies for art projects, taking printer paper and the mini stapler to craft miniature houses and sculptures. But my arms would occasionally press against his calves as he sat in the brown leather swivel chair. And my hands would often brush against his bare feet, which smelled of a long workday in trouser socks and leather shoes. We didn't have to talk; the company was enough.

In that very spot, leaves and dirt are piled high on the floor. The rug is now barely visible. If I look up, I can almost see the sky, the dark, thick bark of a tree trunk obstructing the view. My mom comes in and puts her arms around my shoulders. "I'm sorry, Ash. I hope I didn't upset you. It just feels so violating. This room was like a time capsule for me, a piece of your dad captured forever. Now it's ruined, another part of him taken, without warning."

I hug her, squeezing tight. My heart hurts, too. My dad worked hard to buy this home. He took pride in decorating and even cleaning it. As a kid, I'd wake up on Sunday mornings to him dancing around the living room with a mop in his hands, sweeping to the sounds of Fleetwood Mac or Neil Diamond. Our recollections of him here are priceless, untouchable—until this moment.

I turn around and peek through the open door, catching a glimpse of Dan in the den. He sits, checking text messages, and chills begin to trickle up my arms. He knows how important this house is to my family. Why is he not by my side?

I hold Mom's hand as we face the ruin above our heads. "So many others are in distress. This is fixable, and we're safe. We're lucky." I try to comfort her, and myself, while my annoyance with Dan lingers in the back of my mind.

She gives me a kiss on the cheek. "I know, baby girl, I know."

The following day, I watch as Jill shimmies her slender body into a white gown. The light fabric dances around her feet as she walks, the tulle veil draping her sculpted shoulders, trailing toward her slim waist adorned with a crystal belt, and making its way to the ground where pink rose petals have been sprinkled. The mansion is beautiful, once home to a wealthy Long Island mogul, now a venue for events such as this. The black-and-white-tiled floors complement the grace of grand chandeliers that dangle above winding staircases with soft red carpeting. Floral paintings in heavy gold frames are suspended from the walls, highlighting the breathtaking scale of the room.

Brittney and I lean against a dark wooden chest as we sip champagne and wiggle into our chiffon bridesmaid gowns. I tug on the strapless top of the dress, pulling it higher and adjusting my bra. "Why do these never fit right? No matter how much you spend on tailoring?"

She rolls her eyes. "Tell me about it. How many bridesmaid dresses do you have now?"

I pause, looking up at the sky and counting on my fingers the pastel shades of blue, pink, and yellow that hang in my closet. Worn once and never seen the light of day again. "Gosh, I think I have about eight now, and you?"

Brittney waves her hand in the air. "Twelve! Beat you. But like the bride always says . . . you can cut it short and wear it again."

We both laugh, our glasses clinking together in a cheers as we guzzle the remainder of the bubbles.

Sunflowers and the colors of fall foliage fill the room. Twinkle lights shimmer around large French doors lined with lace curtains and gold tassels. Hours of photographs later, Jill takes her father's hand as they walk toward the center of the dance floor. Jill's dad sways slowly to the music and whispers into her ear. I watch from my chair, my hand rubbing the velvet fabric. I'm happy for Jill, that she's able to have this moment. But I can't help but feel sorry for myself. I try not to be that girl. I know I should be thankful for the blessings in my life. But in this particular department, I feel shortchanged, robbed. The sixteen years I had with my dad don't feel like enough; I want more, more than just the past.

As always, in sentimental moments, my memories intrude. I'm a thirteen-year-old girl at my bat mitzvah, standing in a grand ballroom in a pink raw-silk gown designed just for the day. The sweetheart top curves around my chest, and I twirl around, admiring how the skirt swirls in the air with my spins. The room is covered in pink roses, my favorite. White tulle hangs from the ceilings, curving toward the dance floor and then swooping up, like an optical illusion. A crowd of people in black tuxedos and sparkly gowns surrounds me. But I remain unphased. I hold my dad's hand for a father-daughter dance that we had planned.

Several weeks earlier my dad had said, "Ash, pick a song that we can dance to at your party. Anything that you want."

I instantly knew—it had been playing on the radio and the lyrics were so beautiful. "'Butterfly Kisses,' Dad, that's it!"

He looked at me, confused. "Never heard of it. Why that?"

Years before YouTube and Spotify, I had no way of playing the song for him. "Trust me, Daddy. It's so pretty. You'll understand when you hear it."

He smiled, admiring my persistence, and wrote down the name of the song.

As we slowly danced to the music that cold January evening of my bat mitzvah, the room couldn't have felt warmer. My dad held me close, whispering in my ear, "I get it now, well done." As the minutes passed during our dance, the lyrics told the story of a little girl becoming a teen, and then a woman. Eventually, her father walks her down the aisle as she marries. But her father always thinks of her as a little girl with ribbons in her hair. Dad closed his eyes, and it was as if I could see his imagination run wild. He was picturing me in a white gown, all grown up, giving me away at my wedding. He gave me a kiss. "Baby girl, if you think this party is great, just wait 'til your wedding."

I wipe away the tears now streaming down my face. My heart aches, knowing that he had a dream to see me as a bride, and it'll never come true. Just forty-eight years old when he was killed, and he was already painting a picture of my future. A beautiful life that he wished for me—but with him in it. I hate how he was taken from me so quickly and with such violence. I hate having to see my mom suffer, losing another piece of my dad by a force beyond our control. The lump in my throat seems to grow bigger, and my nerves crank into high gear. Between the memories of my dad and this hurricane, it's clear that life is out of my control, and I feel helpless. I want to be living back in New York with my friends and family. Life is too short not to be near them.

Dan rubs his cheek against mine. "You okay, love?"

I nod as my index fingers trace my eyeliner, wiping away the evidence of tears. "I miss it here. It's home."

He kisses the top of my head. "Me too. Try not to worry. One day, we'll be back."

Ashley, at 5 years old, and, below, at 8, with Dad.

Ashley and her brother Josh, with Dad and Mom. Below,
at her Dad's office in the World Trade Center.

Ashley and Eric on their wedding day.

Jeff Goldflam's inscription at the 9/11 Memorial
Pool, in New York City.

11

There's No Escape

Boston, over the many months I've lived here, has always seemed quaint, with a small-town vibe in a city that otherwise thinks big. But in April 2013 I learn—again— that nowhere is safe.

I'm watching footage of the Boston Marathon. Numbness in my toes travels toward my legs, and my hands begin to tingle. I wipe my fingers against the suede fabric of the sofa, the clammy residue now on the cushion. There's an ache at my temples as the TV leaves nothing to imagination: runners bloodied and injured, patrons running throughout Back Bay seeking shelter, police and ambulances all around. I should feel panic, a fight-or-flight response to the situation. But my past has paralyzed me, preparing me for this kind of reality.

Birds chirp on the fire escape. Their feathers shine in the sun that basks through the open window of my apartment, and a soft breeze is in the air. It's tranquil here, yet I know that twenty minutes away, this city is experiencing the worst moment in its history. My fingers tremble, tightly holding my cell, willing it to ring. Dan's office is near the bombing.

I press on the sticky green button of the phone, redialing repeatedly, and continue being sent to voicemail. Deep inhales of agitation squeeze my lungs, impatience kicking in as I hope for a different outcome with every ring. Why is he not picking up? What if he walked over to the marathon for a quick look? What if he ran out to grab lunch or a coffee and was near one of the bombs? My foot taps on the floor, waiting for any kind of update.

In 2001, my family did the very thing I'm doing right now. Wondering if someone we love made it out alive. I still wonder, did my dad have time to call one of us? Maybe my mom was on the phone and didn't hear the call waiting. Maybe I was in class, cell in my backpack, unable to hear the ring. Although our call history proved otherwise, there's always a bit of doubt in my mind, a game my conscience plays with me for no reason other than to make me sick to my stomach. At this point, maybe it's better not to know.

On the evening of 9/11 I had sat with my mom and brother at the kitchen table. The news had plenty of footage, but all that seemed to play was the same scene of the plane hitting Tower 1, giant red flames and black smoke filling the sky. The plane struck again, and again, and again. Each video clip chipped away a piece of my heart.

I yelled at my brother, "Change the channel! How many times do we have to see this?" Josh held the remote up to the small white television, clicking through the stations. But it was all the same. Plates full of food sat in front of us, no one able to eat.

Josh threw the controller down. "Maybe he made it out. He did during the '93 bombing, remember, Mom? When he worked at that company Fimat?"

At just forty-five years old, my mom looked like she had aged a decade since the news of the attack. Her hair was dry and brittle, her face wrinkled and worn. Her movements were robotic, lacking feeling. She didn't answer him. She stared at the round table, as if searching for answers, trapped in a mental prison we couldn't spring her from. After all, we were just teenagers.

Josh shrugged his shoulders and looked at me, trying to provide comfort. "She's just tired, Ash, don't worry."

He continued flipping through the channels and landed on a station broadcasting people near Ground Zero. They held up pictures of missing family members, crying into the screen, asking viewers to reach out if they have seen their loved one.

Suddenly my mom's eyes widened. "Look!" She ran to the TV. "It's Cousin Sara!"

She had a red bandana around her head and a white tank top covered in dirt. She held two pictures, one in each hand. Her brother-in-law Ben on the left, and my father on the right. Both men had striking blue eyes that seemed to pierce through the camera, grabbing our chests, making it hard to breathe. The signs read: "Jeffrey Goldflam, Tower 1" and "Ben Goldstein, Tower 2." She stared into the camera in agony, helpless and afraid.

My brother dropped the remote control, and the batteries rolled underneath the kitchen cabinets. He looked over at me. "We were just at Ben's wedding. There's no way he and dad could have both been in the buildings, that's insane!"

I stared at my mom, wanting a hug. I yearned for her to hold me and tell me that we would figure this out. But she remained lifeless, unable to reach out. At just sixteen, I knew that she was experiencing a trauma beyond my ability to understand. I wrapped my arms tightly around my chest and gave the best form of comfort to myself that I could.

🦋

While watching the Marathon reports, I notice that my arms, once again, are folded across my chest, trying to provide the same comfort from all those years ago. Suddenly I remember my mother, and an alarm runs through my body. I'm desperate for her to know that I'm safe. If I cause her a second of horror, I'll never forgive myself.

The call goes through, and I hear her calm voice. I'm moment-arily put at ease; she must not have heard about the bombings yet. "Mom! You need to know that I'm safe! I'm in my apartment. There was an attack at the Boston Marathon and people are hurt. The city is chaotic, but I'm okay."

A minute of silence and I'm unsure of her mental state. Have I brought her back to that dark place?

She clears her throat. "Sorry, baby girl. You caught me off guard. It's a sick and scary world we live in. Thank god you're alright. Is Dan with you? Please tell me you're together."

My eyes begin to sting as I hold in tears. Deep down I have to believe that he's okay. That he was at work during the bombing. If that's the case, why hasn't he called? I'm embarrassed to admit to my mom that I haven't heard from him and that I have no idea where he is. The decibels of my voice heighten, attempting to sound strong and unagitated. "I've been waiting almost an hour and haven't heard from him."

From the brief pause and the harsh tone of her voice, I know she's pissed. I get goosebumps down my back and am convinced it's her rage, reaching me hundreds of miles away. "You mean you're alone in that apartment with a terrorist running loose in the city? And your boyfriend, whom you moved for, doesn't bother to reach out and make sure that you're okay? A victim of terrorism yourself? What the hell, Ashley! What is this?"

The sweat dripping from my armpits is proof of the verbal interrogation. I know her heart's in the right place, but I feel judged. In fact, bombarded with judgments. What she's really saying is, "See! I was right! You moved to Boston for someone who isn't in it for the long haul. He wants a girlfriend, not a wife. He doesn't really care about your wellbeing." My imagination plays her voice on repeat as tears roll down my face, not realizing that there's been silence on the line for several minutes.

I cry. "Mom, stop yelling at me! This isn't my fault."

"I'm sorry, Ash." But her sharp tone is a strong indication that she's not sorry. "Dan's supposed to be taking care of you. Where is he at the most pivotal times of your relationship? When you need him most?"

Her points are valid, but it's nothing I need to hear right now; this conversation has to end. "Mom, I have to go. I love you and I'll be in touch soon."

She blows a kiss into the phone, sweet and suddenly supportive. She knows she's pressed the wrong buttons. "I love you. Please bolt the door and stay inside. Call me later."

It kills me to admit that she's right. A pit forms in my stomach, and I pace the apartment, attempting to control my thoughts. My eyes dart to the kitchen and den, examining the pieces that make up my life here. I bend toward the couch, needing to calm my nerves. Dan picked it out on his own, the cushions hard, irritating my back. The sounds of footsteps climbing the walk-up a few feet away play like a melody. Dan chose this apartment building without asking for my opinion. My hand reaches down, caressing my right ankle. An old tennis injury comes to life each day when I climb the flights up to my apartment. Had Dan known or bothered to ask if a three-story walk-up would irritate it? My fingers sweep through a pile of mail on the counter, all addressed to Dan. Would someone even know it's my apartment if they stepped foot in the door? Are there any signs of me in this place? Or in this relationship?

Dan walks in and my body can only manage to walk a few feet toward the door. His footsteps quicken and his muscular arms wrap around my body before I can get a word in. My hands re-main limp at my sides. Dan's head rests between my neck and shoulders. He kisses my cheek and I shiver, as if he's a stranger. He caresses my hair, and I notice the flushed red tone of his cheeks. "I'm so happy you're okay. I was in my office when the bombs went off. Minutes later, police were telling us to evacuate the building and seek shelter. No one knew where to go. I tried to get back here as fast as I could, but the streets were packed with people, all running."

My heart beats hard, and I take deep breaths to control my words. I don't want to sound nervous, but conflict does this to me. "Dan, I called you a dozen times. Why didn't you get back to me?"

He shrugs his shoulders like an elementary school student, called on by the teacher when he doesn't know the answer. "I wish I had an answer for you, but I don't. I was panicked, in shock, really. I didn't think to call."

I step backward, needing space from the stranger in front of me. "My dad died in a terrorist attack. Weren't you wondering if I was okay? Didn't you think I'd want to hear your voice? That I'd need some comfort?"

Dan's fingers comb through the top of his hair, and he lets out a deep breath, frustrated with my anger. "I don't know! I'm not sure about anything right now."

My blood boils, fearing an ultimate betrayal. I find myself shouting as the muscles in my shoulders tighten. "You mean you don't know about us? Or what you want out of this relationship? Do you even want to move back to New York?"

His eyes land on the pile of mail on the counter, and he rummages through several papers. He picks one letter from the bunch, carefully looking it over before handing it to me. His eyes gaze past me, out the dark window framing my back. His embarrassment already permeates the room, and I bite my lip, nervous for what comes next.

The top of the letter has large bold font, the insignia of a prestigious financial institution. I skim the lines—words and phrases like "congratulations" and "looking forward to having you aboard" pop out. It's an offer for a job in New York. The salary is almost double what Dan makes now. The paper travels closer to my eyes, and I blink in disbelief at the date. This was sent three weeks ago. I stutter, catching my breath and organizing my thoughts. "When were you in New York interviewing? Why didn't you tell me?" My composure goes out the window and I run into Dan's arms, kissing his cheeks and neck. "Were you surprising me? I can't believe this!"

He pulls back, shaking his head.

My eyes water, and I pinch my arms, trying to keep in the tears. "You don't want the job, do you?"

He walks away, pouring a dark brown liquor into a small cocktail glass. He slowly sips, looking around the room in search of words. "Ashley, I'm still young. Sometimes I think about backpacking in Europe for a year or taking a job in Asia so I can travel on the weekends. I'm not ready to settle down in one place."

I interrupt abruptly, "Or settle down with one person, is that what you're saying?"

For the first time all night, his eyes meet mine. "Honestly, I'm unsure about everything."

I run, slamming the bedroom door so hard that the floors of the apartment vibrate. I bury my head in the pillows, screaming at the top of my lungs. At twenty-seven, Dan is having a mid-life crisis. He's just ditched the younger woman and sports car for grander ideas of sipping mai tais in Tahiti, void of a job, a lover, and reality.

My heart aches in disappointment, not with Dan, but with myself. What have I been doing my whole life? Not only compromising to be with men I love, but uprooting my life, making changes to the core of the person I am to make a relationship work. I grew up with a father who did everything for his family. He loved my mom and appreciated her strong voice. My parents were a team. I think back through all of my past relationships, realizing I'd been silenced. Where did my voice go? My opinions and what I want? Have I been the woman my dad raised me to be? The answer is crystal clear, and I don't like it one bit.

Do I say what I want when I want it? Do I express my opinions and stand up for them? Because they matter. I realize that I never speak of 9/11, I rarely mention my father, or peel back the layers of the person I've grown to be since sixteen. My words, the most important ones, never see the light of day. I keep the dark feelings inside, the thoughts about terrorism and what happened to me locked up, so no one can see the vulnerability. They can only see the blonde hair and bright smile in front of them.

I sit up and scan the bedroom—the walls of this place appear different now. I examine my face in the dresser mirror, the bags under my eyes and pale skin. My hands press firmly on the counter, gaining balance as my world has been turned upside down, as I realize I'm not happy with the person I've become. My hand drifts toward the knob of the console, opening up a tiny drawer. I grab a small spiral notebook and skim through the pages of daily reminders and doodles. I grab a pen and lean against a corner of the room, my back scraping the wall as I drag myself down to the floor. My fingers begin to move like a dance, ink hits the paper, and the lines fill with words. I'm still figuring out how to find my voice, but for now, I can write. My thoughts and feelings pour out of me like a floodgate that will never again be closed.

Hours later, I blink, and the stiffening pain in my neck radiates to my shoulders. The room is dark, the light from the moon sneaking in the side window, allowing me to see the time on the cable box. It's almost midnight. With the pen and paper still in my hands, I lean on the footboard of the bed, memories flowing through my mind of the earlier events with Dan. It feels like in *The Wizard of Oz* when Dorothy's house has just landed on the ground after being blown through a tornado. Suddenly, I have clarity.

The floorboards creak as I tiptoe toward the den. Dan's body is curled in a ball on the end of the couch. The TV plays in the background as he sleeps. He wakes, startled, and sits up. The slits of his red eyes scan my face for an indication of what comes next.

Has he been crying? Is it bad to say I don't care? I flip on the lights so he can see, leaving no room for misunderstanding. For the first time in my life, I know exactly what I want and how to get there. "I'm moving back to New York. I'll give my two-week notice at the school and will spend that time packing up my things and tying up loose ends here. I'm done." Leaving a class of students mid-term isn't ideal, but if I don't get back to New York soon, I know it will never happen. Dan will lure me back in somehow, and I'll be stuck in a relationship going nowhere.

His body stays glued to the couch and tears flow quickly down his face. "I love you. I don't want you to go."

My hands wave in the air, frustrated and tired. "But you said you don't know what you want. Isn't that right?"

He stares at the cheap brown carpet, unable to admit his confusion.

I turn toward the bedroom, feeling an urge to immediately pack my belongings. Dan follows, observing as I open drawers and pile them messily on the floor next to the closet where the luggage is. I tug aggressively at blouses and pants as they fall from hangers. Then I turn to him. "Get a hotel room, give me space while I make arrangements to move. I'll let you know when I'm gone, then you can come back."

He steps toward me, his right hand extending toward my waist. I quickly shift, and the ice-cold attitude in my eyes tells him not to come any closer. "I don't care if I'm single or for how long. I'm ready to live my life my way. No one will take that away from me ever again."

The mountain of clothes at my feet brings a smile to my face. I'm going home, and I can't seem to get there fast enough.

12

Reality Check

My body sinks into the L-shaped couch, grasping the stem of my wine glass. Perched fifteen flights into the Manhattan sky, an urban starry night twinkles through the windows as switches from adjacent apartment buildings flicker on and off. Even in the late evening, the city bustles as if it's rush hour. Honking horns and street noise drift up and seep through the windows of my brother's apartment. Jill and Brittney sit like bookends alongside me, our feet nestled on the glass coffee table a few feet away.

Jill holds the wine bottle upside down. "We finished another. Ash, where does your brother keep the liquor?"

My head turns toward a cherry-toned wooden chest near the kitchen, and Jill is up before I can get the words out. Brittney multitasks, balancing her glass in between her legs while furiously typing on a small laptop resting on her thighs.

I lean on my right arm, squinting to catch a glimpse of the screen. Brittney firmly pushes my body away. "I'm making your Jdate profile! You can see it when I'm done. You need a little fun, in and out of the bedroom, after that whole Boston debacle."

Jill refills the glasses and shakes her head in disagreement. "Britt, you're so wrong. Ash shouldn't be looking for someone new right now. She just got out of a serious relationship. She needs to recycle, you know, sex with an ex. It's like going through your closet and finding an outfit you've completely forgotten about—try it on again, and it fits great!"

The pinot noir sloshes as I shake with laughter. "Jill, somehow I don't think it's exactly like throwing on an old miniskirt."

Brittney sticks out her tongue with a look of disgust, then, every so often, a nod of approval emerges. "Look at these guys, posting shirtless pictures so the whole world can see their abs. Do they think that's what girls want?"

The three of us stare at a tan six-pack from every angle as Brittney continues to click. Our lips say no but our bodies and minds can't get enough.

The girls gossip about available guys on the dating app—some had been ex-boyfriends, and others they know from college or a random hookup back when they were single. They scream in enjoyment as they point at the faces of men, once in a while saying, "I made out with him once!" or "Oh, that guy, he lives in the apartment next door to me." It's Jewish Geography at its finest; everyone knows each other through the context of sex and dating.

I put my finger over my mouth. "Quiet down! My niece is asleep in the other room. All we need is to wake a three-year-old." I turn toward her bedroom, the silence behind the French doors telling me it's not too late; Jolie's still asleep.

Brittney smiles. "Some babysitters we are, boozing on the couch. Anyway, it's so great that your brother is letting you live here for as long as you want." She observes the modern décor, the spacious open kitchen, and crown moldings on the ceiling. "It really is so nice here, I'd never leave."

I swirl the wine in my mouth, nodding in agreement. "Yeah, I'm lucky I have a support system, or who knows where I'd be living right now. I don't even have a job yet."

Jill lifts the bottle and slips an unnecessary pour into my glass. "Ash, don't pressure yourself. You've been back in New York a month, getting over a breakup. Didn't you say you emailed the principal at your old school in Queens?"

I drink away the disappointment in myself. "She hasn't written back yet. Knowing her, she's looking for a spot for me. She's nice like that."

Jill pats my shoulder. "See, it'll happen, be patient."

My cell phone lights up and I quickly type a message, ignoring the conversation with the girls. Jill grabs it out of my fingers, and I lunge toward her to try and get it back. Then she turns her body so her butt is in my face and the phone is nowhere near my reach. "I want to see who you've been texting, Ash. Who's more important than us?"

I sit back in defeat, awaiting the verbal assault about to come my way. Jill gasps and throws the phone at Brittney. She, too, reads the text message and jumps onto the couch like Tom Cruise's famous interview with Oprah when he says he's in love with Katie Holmes.

Brittney's feet dance up and down on the cushion. "That's why you told us we had to leave! Jason's coming over! You're recycling!"

My arms fold across my chest, covering my body as if they can see right through me. Jill calms herself down. "I know I told you to recycle, but this is insane. Jason messed with your head so much when you were dating. Wasn't he manic-depressive? He'd disappear for days at a time, not show up to dinners. He was unreliable. He made you crazy!"

I stand, collecting their wine glasses like a bartender flicking on the lights in an effort to signal closing time. The girls' honesty is, well, too honest. A little sugar coating never hurt anyone.

As the glasses clink together, I offer a final plea for them to understand. "I have zero desire to get back together with Jason. You said yourself, the name of the game is to recycle. If that's the case, Jason will not disappoint." I look toward the bedroom, day-dreaming of what will be going on in there in an hour or two.

A naughty giggle shoots out of their mouths in unison, like a song. They begin lacing up their shoes and rummaging around the apartment for their jackets. The girls and I partake in a big hug goodbye and I watch as they hit the elevator button. The airy ding fills the hallway and Jill blows a kiss in my direction.

She shouts, "Remember to take your pill!" I hope the neighbors don't hear.

The pitch-black room leaves everything to my imagination. I can't see his light brown hair or slender body, but the power of touch is doing just fine. It's a familiar feeling. I know these lips, I've felt these hands, and it's like an old movie I once enjoyed, being played once again.

Jason's arm wraps around my stomach and I feel his breath against my back. I look up at the ceiling fan as it spins vigor-ously, making me dizzy. Our body temperatures feed off one an-other, so I wrap my legs outside of the sheets. The slight breeze hits my skin and feels refreshing. My fingers trace his, outlining the veins in his hands that lead to his arms. Passion was never the problem here. But I've learned that a good relationship is a package deal. Having lost my dad so suddenly, I crave a steady foundation. A partner who is loyal to the core, someone who can make me feel at ease when the rest of the world seems to be falling apart.

I recall Dan's wide, puppy-dog eyes tearing up when I left Boston. He looked at me for direction, to tell him what to do. Like a little boy, he was lost. But I don't want a boy anymore; I want a man. I no longer say need—I need no one. It's up to me to create my own happiness. A man is just the icing on the cake. My eyelids close, becoming heavy. I nestle my body closer to his and just for tonight, I can enjoy this. Well, maybe tomorrow night, too.

The next morning, the white shades do nothing to keep out the morning light. The perspiration along my legs as they rub together reminds me that I never bothered to put clothes on before bed last night. I swallow slowly. The dry taste in my mouth has remnants of red wine. My head nestles underneath the pillow, my hangover too intense to get up and draw the shades. My body shifts, rolling across the queen-size bed, annoyed to be up so early. Gasping, I throw myself upward, naked torso exposed. I lean across the bed in search of men's clothing and find evidence of last night's rendezvous. But there are no dress pants on the floor. His leather shoes are gone, and there's no wallet or cell phone on the dresser. I fall back into bed in relief. He must have left early this morning. Luckily, there would be no awkward run-in with my niece or, even worse, my brother.

I roll my eyes. What kind of person does this in her sibling's apartment? I'm acting like a post-college graduate, nothing on the mind but martinis and men.

I pull at the blinds, in need of more darkness to match my sudden mood. Behind the thick embroidered fabric is an eleven-by-sixteen framed photo on the wall. I push the curtains aside for a closer look—how have I not noticed this before? The image of a Porsche 911 Carrera grabs my attention. It hung on the wall of my dad's office in our house for as long as I can remember, and it was one of his most prized possessions.

I had been around six years old. It was dark in our driveway, but a small spotlight from the house lights illuminated the front yard. My sparkly pink sneakers pushed hard at the bike pedals, and the rainbow streamers from the handlebars swayed back and forth. My dad was chatting with a man in a suit. They would break from conversation frequently, admiring the Porsche 911 Carrera parked in front. It sat like a fragile artifact in a museum, something to be admired but not touched, especially by small children. I'd cycle past the two men, between their long legs, in hope of some attention. But there was no competition; the sports car won every time.

The stranger handed my dad a pile of papers, which he folded and tucked away in the back pocket of his light-washed Levi's jeans. I'd never seen such a smile on his face before, one of unbridled excitement and joy. It was different from the proud grins he'd throw in my direction when I did a good job with something. Instead, it was clear even to me that this was a day he had dreamed about.

Dad hustled toward the car and slid his body onto the smooth black seat. He inhaled slowly, and from a few feet away, I swear I could smell the scent of fresh leather just by watching him. His hands adjusted the rearview mirror, then wandered to the steering wheel as he caressed the fabric in a soft circular motion.

He looked at the man in disbelief. "I've wanted a car like this since I was a little boy. I worked at a deli in high school to pay for my first car. It was a hippie van, came with curtains and a shag rug on the inside. I'd lend it to my teachers on their lunch breaks, and they'd smoke pot in it."

The man in the driveway adjusted his tie, smiling in admiration of my dad's story.

"You know," Dad continued, "I sold that car in the seventies to buy my wife her engagement ring. So for a while, there was nothing to drive at all."

His eyes studied our home, then scanned his new car, and eventually landed on me. He nodded his head in satisfaction. "Look at my life now. I'm grateful."

The man laughed. "I'm happy for you, Jeff. Just remember this moment when you're stuck in the situation that I'm in right now. When you've got three kids, your wife's hounding you to get a car that can fit the entire family, and you're forced to give this beauty up."

He handed my dad a long roll of paper tied with a rubber band at the center. "The Porsche dealerships give these to every customer. I know you bought the car from me, but the least I could do was have this made for you. I hope you like it."

My dad pulled at the elastic and the poster unfolded, landing at his knees. It was a picture of a candy red Porsche 911 Carrera. The license plate was photo-edited to read "Goldflam." He laughed loudly, tilting the paper so that I could view it. He gently placed the picture in the back seat and turned in my direction, nodding his head, gesturing for me to join him. He threw open the driver's side door and patted his lap. My narrow legs nestled underneath the dashboard. His hands reached down, placing my tiny fingers on the steering wheel. He placed a tape in the radio, and the sounds of Kansas blasted through the garage. The lyrics to "Carry On Wayward Son" echoed off the concrete walls and toward the yard. His mouth made car engine sounds, vrooms and beeps, and he shook his legs furiously, jostling my body as if we were racing down the highway.

This is the poster now hanging on the wall of the guest room, my temporary place of solace. It faces the bed, and it feels as if the Porsche can see everything that I'm doing, watching and judging. I throw a sweatshirt over my head, suddenly feeling like Dad is here and can see me. I look down, ashamed to face my reflection in the framed glass. My stomach aches in embarrassment.

Again, I begin to regret all of the decisions that led me to this place: jobless, apartmentless, and single.

Suddenly, a force greater than myself takes over and I'm shoving my body into yesterday's clothing. I need to get out of here, a reality check to snap out of this wretched place in my mind.

The fly of my pants is still undone as I slam the cab door closed. "Take me to Ground Zero, please. As fast as you can!"

My body bounces up and down as the vehicle hits potholes and stops short at red lights. The open window brings in the smell of the East River's salt water as we drive along the FDR. I made a promise to myself thirteen years ago, when I stood on that wooden platform. As I overlooked the aftermath of the Towers falling, just days after the attacks, I vowed to never step foot there again.

The taxi pulls over. But when I exit, nothing looks familiar. The area has become an epicenter for shopping, with little boutiques, freshly paved roads, and luxurious skyscrapers. Oak trees line the street and moms push strollers to a nearby school. The dust and rubble have been replaced with manicured lawns and bustling sidewalks. I shake my head in confusion. Am I in the right place?

A walking bridge connects the east side of the street to the west. Miniature American flags protrude from the grass. I follow the path, and my feet move quickly, almost running toward the other side. My muscles are tied in knots, feeling the need to be where my dad last stood.

The marble floors of the walkway lead to hard brown ground. Dust from dried mud covers the front of my boots, the land now barren. A large, tarnished fence stretches endlessly, enclosing the perimeters of what was once Tower 1. I can feel the uneven, rusty surface against my shirt as my body presses against the metal. My fingers poke through the holes of the barricade, yearning to be on the other side. An incredibly large concrete square is visible—the foundation of the Tower. It's now hollow, filled with the dreams and souls of those who lost their lives too early. Voices never able to tell their stories, to hug their families one more time. The emptiness is somehow palpable, and my heart aches.

Construction workers operate machines, yet the shrills never pierce my ears. I hear nothing, just the sound of my cries, all from within. From time to time the workers in yellow hard hats glance in my direction, staring for a moment before continuing to drill. They must know by now the difference between a tourist and a victim. Some make eye contact, nodding their heads, paying me their respect.

I realize that my dad wouldn't want me standing here, alone and sad. He wouldn't be ashamed of my behavior. Nor would he even care that I moved to Boston, just to leave and come right back to New York with no success in love or career to speak of. What he would be mad at, furious with even, is my perspective. The disappointment I feel toward myself. This place, which was once a horrendous war zone left to fire, smoke, and ash, is a reminder, a reality check that I so need. The Towers may no longer be here, but I am.

13

That Girl

In a SoulCycle no-no, I lift my wrist to reveal the time: seven a.m. I wish away the minutes of class, needing a break from the pain—not to mention the panic of getting to work on time. A few teachers went on maternity leave over the summer, opening up a position for me. My calves ache, divine exhaustion at its finest. My toes curl downward, the tiny muscles tense. The slow R&B rhythm is like a guide, indicating how my body should move. The burning in my thighs intensifies as my butt pushes forward and back, left to right. The thick smell of sweat in the air washes over me as perspiration slowly drips from my neck to my chest.

I catch a glimpse of myself in the large mirror against the wall, front and center in a sea of passionate, pedaling women.

I pat myself down with a damp cloth as I exit class. Jill nudges my arm. "Well, we've officially burned enough calories to drink all we want tonight."

My stomach aches in excitement and nervousness about our ten-year high school reunion. "Do you think this workout was enough to squeeze into that black miniskirt I bought a while back?"

Jill laughs, shaking her head in a way that tells me I need a lot more than one cycling class to do the trick.

The stark white locker room is packed with women. Long legs meander toward the showers. I squeeze the sticky shirt over my head and quickly grab a towel to cover up. I blush and turn toward Jill. "Public nudity is not my thing."

Jill throws her sports bra on the ground, then stares herself down in an adjacent mirror. I point to her breasts, in awe of the size. "Put those things away! This is a place of business."

She pushes my arm and laughs. "Don't judge!"

We step into adjoining showers, continuing our conversation through the gap near the ceiling. The sound of water smacks against the tiled floor, making it hard to hear. Luckily, Jill has the loudest voice in Manhattan.

I scrub my body, attempting to mentally put together an outfit for tonight. "So what are you going to wear?"

The *hmm* of Jill's voice hints that she's ditching her usual patches, suede, and hippie garments for something different. "I think a cute black dress, short and sexy." She pauses. "We've got to look good, show the ex-boyfriends what they missed out on!"

I silently agree, feeling the pressure. I'm already showing up shorthanded, the only single person in our group of friends. No hot guy to show off as arm candy and no apartment to call my own. The only positive tidbit about my life is that I'm working. Am I making millions? Far from it. Am I successful? In my mind, not losing one of my thirty students at the end of the day qualifies as a win. But to others, will it be enough? My ribs tighten, and a stiffness forms in my chest.

I worry about what my old peers will be thinking. They all saw me running through the halls on 9/11. They were all at my father's memorial service as I spoke, trying to get the words out before the tears came. They saw my struggle. My worst fear is their thoughts. *What ever happened to that girl whose dad died? Was she ever able to be normal? How could someone be normal after that?*

I turn the water to cold, and it slaps my face. Gasping loudly, I refuse to accept those ideas.

Jill and I part ways outside the gym, giving kisses goodbye as if we won't be seeing each other in ten hours. She waves as she crosses the street. "Get ready for some fun—girls' night out, baby!"

Two subway rides later, I sit behind my desk as my Gifted and

Talented fifth graders are hard at work. It's my favorite time of year. Pumpkins line the shelf underneath the Smartboard at the front of the room. Scarecrows and plastic leaves in brown, green, and orange dangle from the doorway, outlining the lofty ceiling of the classroom.

I know I shouldn't do it, but I just can't help myself. I sneak my phone out from the desk drawer, holding it low and out of sight. My fingers click on the app and a slew of emails pop up, messages from the latest Jdaters. I reread my dating profile, embarrassed by the honesty. I skim through, keywords jumping out from the screen: looking to establish roots and stay in New York, want someone to share my life with, not looking for a fling. Well, any player who reads this will certainly go running for the hills— I know I would. I sigh, clicking on the email tab to see who's reached out. At least I'm being bold, putting out there what I want.

Laughter fills the air and students look over in my direction. The disgusted expression on my face must be a dead giveaway. How many men, old enough to be my father, are going to contact me? To make it worse, they ask for photos of my legs or other body parts. Hello, weird! I delete creepy messages, one after the other, until I reach one that seems promising. The man looks to be in his mid-thirties and is cute. His email is polite and sweet. He wants to know more about me, where I'm from, where I went to college, what I do for a living. All the normal get-to-know-you stuff. Is it worth writing back? I zoom in on his profile.

His username is "ebiz." Looks like his name is Eric. He's a Giants,

Yankees, and Rangers fan. He mentions his little white Westie and love of family. Another finance guy. Maybe I should go for something new this time? Then again, a person's job doesn't define who they are. He's tall with jet-black hair and has dark olive skin.

To save time, I copy and paste an email back to him. One that I've sent to a bunch of other guys who all asked similar questions. It's easier this way. I've learned my lesson about spending too much time emailing or texting with a man I've met online. They seem perfect, and hours have been spent exchanging pleasantries back and forth. Then we meet in person a few weeks later and disaster hits. In their profile picture they have a full head of hair. In reality they show up to the date bald.

That evening, I step into a dark bar hoping I'll meet a guy the old-fashioned way. Pushing the heavy glass doors open, the space is brightened by amber accent lights and black couches. A nineties playlist echoes against the walls, mixed with loud voices from the crowd. My eyes scan the faces in the room, and it's like a dream. The people I grew up with haven't aged a day. The only noticeable difference seems to be our wardrobes: sweatpants and white T-shirts have been replaced with business suits and wedding rings.

I take a deep breath and run over to Brittney, spotting her sequined black Gucci bag from a mile away. The exaggerated hellos and squeals of women I haven't seen in a decade blur the music. It feels like a game of spin the bottle where I'm forced to kiss and hug everybody in my path. Maybe at one point in my past I did? It was high school, who can remember?

The girls take turns bragging about recent promotions, engagements, and new homes. They fuss about big mortgages and when to start trying for a baby.

Laura Bernstein talks. Her hair, which was once long and frizzy, now softly sways down to her shoulders. We were in Hebrew school together and she was always an overachiever. Perfect grades, sweet as pie to everyone, the body of a dancer, thin and graceful. I was fond of her. Who wasn't? On our graduation day the principal stood at the podium and delivered a ten-minute speech about overcoming obstacles. He had a trophy in his hand and was about to grant it to the student who persevered through incredible challenges during their high school career. He called Laura's name and awarded it to her for battling a bad case of mono. Well then, that certainly must have been in the same category as losing a parent to terrorism.

She glances in my direction, nudging my elbow. "Ashley, what have you been up to all these years? You look great."

I assume she's referring to the ten pounds I lost since my recent breakup. As her lips move, the words begin to fade. The noise in the room drifts into a haze of silence, and the stares from the brown eyes that surround me make my heart beat fast. The looks of old friends and acquaintances burn through me, and I wonder which episode from my past plays in their minds. Which 9/11 story do they remember most?

As a junior in high school, I'd sit with my SAT tutor in the local library twice a week, nodding as he taught math tricks for the big test. I didn't understand a word he said but was too scared to admit it. He'd think I was stupid, dumb for not knowing the answers. Looking back, I know that the only stupid question is the one not asked.

My SAT exam was a month after 9/11, and I felt an intense burden to do well on it. A different reason from all the other kids who wanted to get into an Ivy League college or impress people with the abundance of acceptance letters they'd received. For me, it was my only shot to get out of New York. To pick a school far away where no one knew my last name or about my past. I wanted to be in a place where people only knew about my link to 9/11 if I chose to tell them, if they were given that privilege. Here, in New York, the words "Goldflam," "Cantor Fitzgerald," and "death" all went hand in hand. I felt like a freak, people studying my every movement, wondering how I could still function after going through what I did. So I had to score well.

I no longer wanted to be "that girl" who ran through her high school to get to a phone that Tuesday morning. The girl who everyone must have judged in one way or another. Whether it was pity, empathy, sympathy, or sorrow. This was my chance to take control of my life and make a change. And that, I had thought, would never happen if I went to a New York college.

On the day of the test, I sat in a small, creaky wooden seat, one where the desk was attached to the chair by a thin metal rod. The classroom looked like any other: concrete white walls with a large green chalkboard at the front. This high school, chosen to be the testing center for the day, was the place where my fate would be determined. The muscles in my stomach began to tighten, and I scanned the room looking for a friend, some reassurance that everything would be okay.

I suddenly spotted a black poster behind the teacher's desk. It seemed larger than life, almost engulfing the entirety of the plain wall. It had a red, white, and blue background. Front and center was the silhouette, black and ghostly, of the Towers. In large font above the image read: NEVER FORGET. The antenna of Tower 1 grabbed my attention, and it was impossible to focus on anything else. The students sitting around me witnessed my blank stare. They noticed that my pencil remained lifeless, sitting on top of my paper. It was evident that I'd need a lot more than this test to get me into college. I'd need a miracle.

🦋

The same faces from that day now give me the same gaze, poised for an update on my life. All the same people are waiting to see what "that girl" will do next. How will I react? Given my unfortunate circumstances.

Like an old projector, flashes of memory scroll through my

mind, one after the next. Now a vision of a tall and intimidating police officer comes into focus.

W

It was the end of senior year. Two weeks left until graduation and freedom. We sat, sweat dripping from our bodies in the hot social studies classroom. A guest speaker was coming in to give a lecture on the future. I doodled pictures in my notebook while Jill and Brittney gossiped and passed notes. The giggles and snickers of giddy teenagers ready to let loose resounded.

I jolted in my seat when the classroom door quickly opened: a police officer walked in, slamming the bulky wooden handle behind him. The floor shook, along with our bodies. His thick, dark hair was slicked back, accentuating his chiseled jawline and intense eyes. He moved slowly, scanning the classroom, examining each student as if we had just committed a felony. His large right hand held on to his brown leather belt, next to his handcuffs and gun. His slow, deliberate steps were unnerving, his silence intimidating.

He picked up the white chalk, writing his name on the board. "Class, I'm Mr. McKinley. I'm here to remind you of how lucky you are, how fortunate every person in this room is." His eyes traced the designer pocketbooks hanging from the girls' chairs and the fancy running sneakers tied to the boys' feet. He shook his head in disapproval.

"You've been privileged, raised in an affluent neighborhood without a care in the world. You're about to go to college, and this is not reality, my friends. You need to be prepared for the cruel world that awaits you out there."

I straightened my back, every muscle and tendon tied in knots, afraid the officer would call on me or ask me a question. Petrified to turn my head in any direction, my eyes darted around the room. The tension in my body was reflected in the faces of my peers, all afraid, knowing we were being judged too quickly.

I became furious, the feelings of fear turning to anger. My fists clenched and teeth grinded, my jaw tight and locked. How dare this man come into our school, our home, and judge us. My friend Rachel sat beside me. Her dad died of Agent Orange poisoning in Vietnam, her mother not long after from a broken heart. Did the fancy blouse covering her emotional wounds make her a bad person? On my other side was Pam. Her mother was living in a mental institution. Every day she came to school with a pout on her face, a loneliness I could feel every time she moved, in every word she spoke. Did the expensive soccer cleats on her feet make her any less vulnerable?

A shout startled me, bringing my attention front and center. My arms became numb as the officer's eyes threw daggers into me. He yelled, "I noticed you looking off into the distance, miss. You don't care about what I have to say?"

I couldn't find a response. The words were all in my head, dancing around and bursting to see the light of day. But instead, I was speechless. He approached my desk and placed his hands wide, leaning down so our eyes were level. "Young lady, when you sit at graduation in a few weeks, you should be thankful. Appreciative that you have family there to watch you receive your diploma. You must learn to be grateful; not everyone has that."

My heart felt as if it had stopped beating. Like I'd been shot, right in the chest, and I wished I could fall to the floor and disappear. My classmates' jaws dropped. My shoulders quivered, mortified and embarrassed to be exposed so openly. At that moment, I knew that all twenty-five classmates were thinking the same thing: *Her dad won't be there.*

My face fell into my hands and I couldn't stop crying. My plastic chair was in the middle of everyone. For what seemed like minutes on end, I sobbed into my palms as everyone watched, no one knowing what to do to help.

The officer put his hand on my right shoulder; I can still feel the heat in my body rising toward his touch. I wanted to hit him, to take his arm and break it off. But I couldn't. He whispered in my ear, "Whatever your loss was, I'm truly sorry."

The last thing I remember is Jill walking toward my seat, her arm around my shoulder as she talked me out of a spiral tizzy. "You're okay, Ash, you'll be okay."

Jill's arm is around mine once again, her cheery, loud voice radiating through the bar. Pure relief calms my nerves, the stress in my shoulders lifting.

It dawns on me, like a baby opening its eyes and witnessing the world for the first time. It's as simple as can be and I wish I had realized this sooner. It's just three words, but in the moment, it's everything: *I don't care.*

If all people see is blonde hair and a pretty smile, I pity their inability to peel back the layers. If all they see is a victim, then they can't recognize what it looks like to pick yourself up and dust yourself off. No one—the terrorists, the public, old acquaintances—holds the power to define me. I choose to define myself. I am and will forever be "that girl." That girl who refuses to break. That girl who will unapologetically live a life without limits. That girl who owns with confidence her actions, body, and mind. I'm that girl my mom and dad raised, and I'll wear that title proudly.

14

Out of Retirement

The reunion is a success, a long night of reminiscing that ends in the early morning hours. I rub my eyes and stumble out of bed, heading toward the kitchen for coffee. My mom sits with Josh at the round wooden table, quietly talking. Jolie is beside them with a plate of pancakes, eagerly holding the syrup in the air as liquid slowly oozes onto her plate.

I give Mom a kiss on the cheek. "When did you get in? I didn't know you were coming today."

She pats the cushion on the chair beside her where a toasted bagel is waiting for me. Her clenched jaw reveals a look I am all too familiar with, and I know she's not here for a fun shopping day. Josh's foot taps on the floor as he looks to my mom for direction.

I hold a warm mug tight, sipping slowly. "Just say it already.

What's going on?" But their mouths stay screwed shut, and their eyes lock with one another, unable to face me.

Unable to control my annoyance, I put down my mug on the table so firmly that the coffee spills over. "I'm twenty-eight years old! I can handle it. And no offense, I'm the one who deals with these things the best. You two are so emotional."

Josh squints his eyes. "You think you could handle knowing half the stuff we do about 9/11? We keep things from you to protect you."

My mom remains speechless. I'm now the black sheep of the family. I have inherited my dad's sarcasm, and his ability to compartmentalize feelings and put on a tough act when necessary. Josh and my mom, they wear their hearts on their sleeves. I call them emotional cutters. They sit on bad news, dwell on it as it eats them alive.

I snap back at Josh. "So what is it this time?"

Mom cuts us off, annoyed with the sibling rivalry. "Some people working on the memorial museum called. They want us to come to their office and tell stories about Daddy. They will record it; those tapes will be played in the museum when it opens sometime in the spring."

The little black lines that run through the beige marble floor catch my eye. They spread throughout the tiles like veins on an arm, and I get goosebumps as I try to distract myself.

Mom's French-manicured nails tickle my hand, grabbing my attention. "Ash, will you come with us? To talk about Dad? They only allow three people; it should be us."

I quickly shake my head without having to think. "No. There's no way I'm doing that. My memories with Daddy aren't entertainment for the public. I'm not here to be on display so people can pretend they know what my life is like or what I've gone through. Keep me out of it."

The moment feels like déjà vu from a few years ago when we were asked to send family photographs to the museum. I didn't want my face there. Now I don't want my voice there, either. When 9/11 first happened, I wasn't given a choice about how to grieve or whom to mourn with. I had never felt so exposed, so naked to the world. Everyone thinking they knew how I felt, asking if I wanted to talk. All I wanted was to be alone. To hide out, cry in secrecy, scream into my pillow, and hope that one day it would all just pass.

Why do I have to be the person to spill my guts? Why should I open up my heart and show my wounds to complete strangers? It's so one-sided. It's not fair for people to know everything about me when I know nothing about them.

Josh argues, "Ashley, this museum will be here until the end of time. It will encapsulate us. It's a place where Jolie and, one day, your children can visit. Our grandchildren and great-grandchildren will have the incredible opportunity to see their history and know where they came from."

I get up, pushing in my chair as a non-verbal closure to the conversation. "You make it sound like Ellis Island. It's the place where dad was killed—not the same thing."

Why doesn't my family understand me? Why don't they see my side? My body grows hot in frustration, feeling alone and defeated. Just like that, my decision is made, and it isn't brought up again.

In December, I sit at the vanity in my bedroom, applying makeup. Jolie studies every movement, then replicates it. Her little fingers grasp the pink palettes of blush, dabbing her cheeks and eyelids. She then picks up the lip gloss and applies a smooth red layer to her delicate mouth, blotting one too many times before striking a vogue-like pose in the mirror.

My cell phone, placed on the mirrored dresser, rings, and I press the speaker button. My mom's voice makes an attempt to be cheery on the other end. "Hi, Ash! Getting ready for your big date?"

I roll my eyes in annoyance. "Mom, this is why I usually don't tell you when I'm going to meet someone. You make such a big deal! It's so much pressure."

She sighs. "Oh, lighten up. Anyway, I have to say something. You were right about not wanting to do the tape recording for the museum. I went a few days ago, and it's been a really hard week since."

My heart feels crushed, wishing I could take away some of the pain she carries. "Oh, Mom, why did you do it? You don't have to say yes to all these things."

She sniffles and catches her breath. "I'm doing it for Daddy, to keep his memory alive. I had to go to this office building downtown. They took me into a tiny dark room, and it was sweltering. Can you believe that? In the middle of winter and the heat was blasting so hard that I broke into a sweat. Anyway, I had a tiny bottle of water and was asked over and over different questions about Daddy, how we met, our wedding, our life together."

I blink several times, hoping the tears will go away. I say nothing. If I even attempt to console her, I think I'll lose it.

"The lady interviewing me was trying to be nice, I could tell," she continues. "But it was obvious she had done this a hundred times before. Day after day, she sits in that sad room and records stories about the victims who were killed. She looked depressed, and who could blame her? It made the process that much more excruciating."

"So was it worth it? Would you do it again if you had the choice?"

She fights back without hesitation. "I would do it again in a second. I think, in time, you may wish you did the recording. But for now, to relive the heartbreak over and over again, I'm glad that you removed yourself from the situation. You're strong, and you know what's best for yourself."

Tears roll down my cheeks, but I refuse to give in to the emotion. If I'm sad, my mom's sad, and I can't do that to her. Like a vacuum, I suck in all of the sorrow and tuck it away. "Mom, I love you. I'll text you from the date and let you know if it's a complete disaster."

I end the call, noticing the time, and run to the closet. I pull a loose black turtleneck off the hanger and throw it over my head. It's my first-date sweater, my go-to outfit when I meet someone new. I learned my lesson a while ago, after meeting a guy I connected with online at a bar while wearing a slinky black halter top. I don't know if it was the blonde hair or my wardrobe choice, but he treated me like a complete ditz. I'll never forget when he asked, "I used to work downtown, right near the World Trade Center. You know what that was, right?"

I threw on my jacket and ran out the door. I promised myself I'd never feel that uncomfortable again. So all my future dates can thank that idiot for my first-date outfit of choice, the pilling, baggy, unflattering black turtleneck.

Felice 64, a local wine bar that Eric, ebiz, suggested, sits on a quiet corner of the Upper East Side. As I cross the street, the cold air travels up my coat, raising goosebumps along my back. A man waits by the front door of the restaurant and instinctively I know it's him. Fresh out of work, he's wearing a dark business suit. He looks exactly as his pictures described, with dark hair and skin. Even in the middle of winter, he seems to have a tan.

His head turns from side to side, looking for me.

I approach him, and his bright smile is sincere. I lean forward for a friendly hug. "Hi! It's so nice to meet you!" His right hand stays against my back and he ushers me toward the door.

"I already got us a table inside, I hope that's okay."

Eric takes my coat; my hands immediately pat down the lumpy black sweater hiding my body. Now I wish I wore a different outfit. He sits down, looking over the menu. A thick candle rests between us on the wooden table, illuminating our faces in the otherwise dark room. "Would it be okay if I ordered a bottle of red?"

I smile as he quickly orders. He clears his throat. "So you're from Long Island, too. Funny, we've never met before. Do you go home often?"

He leans close to the table, ignoring the banter from people beside us. I take a small sip of wine. "I'm there all the time. Usually visiting my mom. I also love Montauk. It's my favorite place in the whole world."

His eyes widen. "I've been there once or twice. Why is it special for you?"

My memory drifts to the smell of salt water and large waves. My dad's hands lifting me over the tide. "My family goes at the end of every summer. Well, we used to go, back when I was a kid. It was different in the eighties. It was simple there—just a beach, pizza place, and an ice cream shop. Montauk was a quaint little town, and my dad loved going there because it was an escape from the city."

I catch myself saying the word "dad" and instantly stop talking. I didn't want to open up that door. This is always the part of the date when my heart beats a little faster. Searching for the right words, assessing how vulnerable I want to be. I procrastinate, gazing at other couples seated at the tiny wooden tables, underneath the dimly lit modern chandelier on the ceiling.

Eric refills my glass, studying my eyes as I watch his pour. "Tell me about your family. What are your parents like? Do you have siblings?"

I decide to give him the answer I tell all men I meet. It's easy, uncomplicated. "My dad's retired and I have an older brother, he's your age actually."

What's the alternative thing to say if someone asks about my dad? To tell the truth would be exposing the most vulnerable part of myself. What if I think I can trust a guy and then he decides he's no longer interested in me? I'd have put my heart on the line just for it to be broken. The core of my being exposed. This is why I want no part in the museum. It gives people the opportunity to have an opinion about my life, to provide their thoughts and unsolicited opinions.

But now, for the first time ever, I feel differently. I wish I could take back the words I've just said to Eric. Deep down in my stomach, I know he's worth the risk. There's something about his demeanor, the way he studies my words when I speak. He stops whatever he's doing when I reply to a question. He genuinely wants to hear what I have to say. And I've just lied.

The server approaches. "Pardon the interruption. I see you two are engrossed in conversation. Is there anything else I can get you?"

I want so badly to stay. Eric looks to me for approval, his cheeks becoming rosy once again. He scans the menu. "We'll have the charcuterie plate." He turns toward me. "I hope I'm not keeping you captive, but I'm not ready to leave."

I can't even look into his eyes, fearful he will see right through me. How intrigued I am by him, how attracted I feel.

He continues the conversation. "Did I mention that I have a brother, too? He's younger, though, so I always feel like I need to protect him. Even though he's married with children and doesn't need me anymore."

He looks down at the candle in the center of the table, his sudden silence revealing his mind at work, going back in time, I imagine, to days of playing catch on the front lawn, keeping a close eye on his brother as his father instructed him to do.

I laugh, thinking of Josh and his overwhelming need to protect my mom and me. "You and my brother would have a lot in common. I actually live with my brother right now, and I think he truly wants me to stay there indefinitely. Every time I search for an apartment he says, 'Stay for a few more months. We're having so much fun.'"

Eric grins. "Don't give him a hard time, he's just looking out for you. So this relationship you were in, the one you mentioned earlier, from Boston. You lived with the guy?"

My palms begin to sweat a little. The thought of Dan makes me cringe, like I'm tainted in some way. I had already placed my dream of living with someone and my hope for a proposal in the wrong hands. Will Eric use this as some sort of red flag to think I'm not good with relationships or men? I search his face for an answer.

His head tilts to the side and shakes. "I'm sorry. That must have been horrible. It could've been worse—at least you didn't marry the guy. You dodged a bullet."

His sympathetic voice puts me at ease. My shoulders slink downward, and it feels like a ton of bricks have been lifted. I don't need defenses with him. I feel I can be myself. The dim flame from the candle between us repeatedly flickers. Its wick bubbles and melts down, a small clump of wax sticking to the table. The fire burns out, revealing that time has passed all too quickly.

The waiter stands beside us with an apologetic smile. "Pardon the interruption. I just want to let you know that we will be closing shortly. It seems like you two should set up a cot in the back and stay, but unfortunately we can't accommodate that."

With one look, Eric's eyes meet mine. We both laugh, thinking the same thing. Lying on a cot together doesn't sound half bad. We stand, Eric holds up my jacket, and I turn my back toward him as he slips the fabric over my body. "I can't believe we were sitting here for five hours. I'll walk you home."

I admire the sparkly colored lights on the storefronts as we stroll down First Avenue. The Christmas décor lights up an otherwise dark sky. Evergreen trees still line the street, waiting to be sold, a final attempt to bring in holiday cheer. The frost in the air as I exhale makes me shiver, and I keep my hands buried in my pockets for warmth.

Eric tells me about his family and growing up. How his father took him to every Giants and Yankees game imaginable. There's a melancholy look on his face as he explains how his father would try to sneak him into games without having to pay, but the attempt failed every time. There's something off here, a secret in between the lines. Sometimes he talks about his dad in the past tense and then will switch to present. I know this part of grief—I'm guilty of it, too. It's a defense mechanism. Fighting with your own brain and reality, not wanting to admit that the person you love is no longer here.

I take Eric's hand and stop walking. I stand close, looking into his chocolate brown eyes. "Your dad passed away. Am I right?"

He looks down, takes a deep breath, and nods. "He had cancer, battled it for so many years. How did you know?"

I can feel the cold air hit my face, and the small tip of my nose reddens. "I'm sorry I didn't tell you the truth earlier. My dad died, on 9/11 actually."

His pointer finger gently touches my lips. "You don't owe me an explanation."

We look into each other's eyes, and in a moment where nothing is said, we know everything we need to. We are both part of the club. It's not a place anyone wants to be, but once you're there, it instantly connects the people in it. It's clear we both miss our fathers and can't help but discuss them. We're proud of the adults we've become because of them. Have I finally met some-one who understands me, and my story?

Eric's arms wrap around my body and just like that, our lips press together. He holds me tight. Then he eventually pulls away and whispers in my ear, "Thank god I got the chance to hold you. I didn't know what was underneath that baggy sweater."

We both laugh and I make a promise to myself. On the next date, I'll leave little to his imagination.

15

The Only Palm Trees in New York

A strong breeze travels across my bedroom, caressing my face. The cool air of April is a pleasant reminder that spring break is approaching. My body twirls, spinning halfway, examining my curves that fill a bright, patterned bikini. My feet glide above the fabric of other swimsuits and cover-ups not making the cut and thrown to the floor. There isn't much room in my new tiny studio apartment on the Upper East Side. The third floor permits the loud honking of traffic and street chatter to drift above into the space. I look around, appreciating the privacy. As I throw flip-flops and beach bags into an old suitcase I smile, remembering a conversation Eric and I had weeks ago in this very spot.

It was late February, and I was out to dinner celebrating my twenty-ninth birthday. Eric understood it was a girls' night out but couldn't help but remind me that I was on his mind. He sent two bottles of champagne to our table with a special note. I'll never forget the look on my friends' faces. They were excited to drink for free and in shock that my new boyfriend would take the time and energy to visit the restaurant hours earlier. He picked out the perfect liquor and attached a handwritten note.

Jill had yelled that night, "Eric's totally your future husband! He's going to propose." I ignored her silly comment. After all, we had only been dating a month at that point. But deep down, I had a feeling that something was different in this relationship.

That night Eric slept at my apartment so I could give a proper thank-you for the surprise. As a birthday gift, he handed me an envelope with two tickets to the Dominican Republic. "I booked the vacation for April, if that's okay. It's when we'll get the best beach weather in Punta Cana."

No one had ever done something like this for me before. Eric was a true planner. We never left a date without him asking me out for another night, with a dinner reservation or event already in mind. In this case, he went over the top, planning a long weekend away on an exotic beach at a hotel called The Sanctuary. My face flushed when I realized what he had done. I jumped up in bed, forgetting I was naked, bouncing up and down in excitement. He was amused at the spectacle, but I wish I had put clothes on before doing that happy dance.

Still, thrilling as it was to have received such a generous gift, I knew I couldn't accept it. My dad always said that he worked hard so that I didn't have to ask anyone for anything. As I got older, my mom continued to instill this perspective in me. When

I went off to college, she always made sure I had enough money in my pocket so that I could buy my own drinks at the bar and didn't have to borrow money from friends. She never wanted me to be the girl who needed a man to buy her a cocktail. I always felt guilty for having extra cash, telling Mom I'd get a job in college for extra spending money. She refused every time. In her mind, I had grown up too fast, and college was the time to study hard and also have a little fun.

I was thinking back to those conversations with my parents when I offered to pay Eric back for the trip. He said no every single time. One day I took a neatly folded check and left it on his desk. It was never cashed, but at least I tried. There was a side of me that had difficulty letting him take the financial reins with this trip. Would I owe him something? Would I now be forced to act a certain way or say thank you a thousand times? I told myself to stop taking life so seriously. It's just a trip with a man I think I'm falling in love with.

Now I eagerly pack my bags, amazed that time has gone so fast. Our flight leaves early tomorrow morning, and it can't come any sooner. I sift through cover-ups and flirty dresses, examining what's sexy and cute enough to make the trip. I fold clothes, daydreaming of the warm sun. My cell rings and I quickly press the speaker button, too busy to see who it is.

"Hi, Ash, it's Dan." The voice on the other end startles me. Is this real? I try to piece together the reason for the call, unable to respond.

"Listen, I moved back to New York. I made a mistake letting you go."

It sounds like he followed me here. But I know better. If that were the case, he'd already be at my doorstep. He would have tracked me down through friends or family in desperation to win me back. Instead, all I get is a measly phone call in a pathetic attempt for reconciliation. This isn't a man in love. This is a boy, confused and lonely, and probably horny.

"Dan, why are you in New York?"

He answers quickly. "I ended up taking that job offer, more money, a bigger city. The company I'm at also has offices around the world, so I can travel, even relocate one day."

My arms shake, anger flushing through my spine and down to my legs. Is he crying? Do I hear tears? This isn't about me. Nothing he ever did was because of me, and this is just another example. "Dan, you had your chance. You watched me leave Boston and didn't do a thing to stop me. You basically helped pack up my boxes. You want me because you're alone and too lazy to put yourself back out there. You just need someone, anyone."

I don't want to be on this call another minute. What if he says something to pull me back in? I know he's not the one for me. I know he doesn't really care about my feelings. I take a deep breath. It would be so easy to go back to him. At least I know what I'm getting. But I know settling is the simple answer, not the right one. What can I say to get him out of my life? "Listen, I'm dating someone. It hasn't been that long but it's kind of serious, and I really think it's something special. So please, leave me alone."

Shocked, he cuts me off. "Babe? Who is he? Do you really think you're going to marry this guy? Don't be ridiculous. Come back to me."

I want to make some witty comment. Something that breaks his heart as much as mine was broken when I took that last train ride back to New York. But I can't do it. I'm genuinely happy. And as much as he's hurt me, I want him to find solace in his life. What I know for sure is that I'm not the answer for him. He doesn't love himself yet, making him incapable of loving anyone else.

"I'm not your babe, don't call me that. And this may sound crazy, but yes, I think I'm going to marry this guy. So please, lose my number."

I hang up before he can get in another word. My body falls to the floor, surrounded by beachwear and a large suitcase. I examine the clothing, scanning the sunglasses and flip-flops on the ground. Each trinket representing a dream. A wish for my future, hopefully with Eric. He takes care of me, mentally and emotionally, in a way I never knew was possible. But marriage? Is that really where I think this is headed? My stomach turns nervously, afraid of disappointment.

What if this doesn't work out? What if Eric turns out to be like other guys I've dated? They were intrigued with me in the beginning, too, but then became unavailable. They realize they're too immature, not ready for a serious relationship. Or they wonder if they can find someone more attractive, smarter, wittier. In Manhattan, a place of limitless people and possibilities, the grass is always greener. I don't think Eric is that kind of guy. But this relationship is still new, and how well do I really know him?

I'm approaching thirty, a scary age for most women. My girlfriends have placed a high bar on this number. It's when we should have it all figured out: marriage and children, the indicator of whether "she" leads a happy and successful life. But after Dan, I realized that being with him would be like cheating at the game of love. Like cutting corners in a race. I'd rather be single, happy, and enjoying my life well into my thirties than in a mediocre relationship, pretending it's something that it's not.

The following day and a quick plane ride later, we are in the Dominican Republic. Eric and I hold hands as we walk the gray cobblestone trail toward the hotel. Lush gardens surround the path, guiding us toward white cottages with orange Spanish roofs. The friendly staff, mostly male, wave at us and shout greetings. Some come close, calling me J.Lo, then head back to work. I turn to Eric, embarrassed by the remarks. Should I be offended or happy that the men see a resemblance between myself and one of the most beautiful women in the world? Even though I know the reference is about the back of my body, not the front.

Eric considers the thought. "Maybe they're calling *me* J.Lo?"

I burst out laughing. "In your dreams!"

Escorted into our private villa, a dark wooden four-post bed is in the center of the room. A sheer beige canopy drapes down the four corners. Open glass sliding doors encourage the salty smell of ocean air to drift in. The expansive turquoise water stretches toward the horizon. I quickly unzip my suitcase and begin throwing off my clothes. "Let's get out there! We only have five more hours of sun!"

Eric lunges onto the plush white bedding, throwing the red rose petals off to the floor. "Exactly, its only noon. Slow down, we'll get there."

I smile, realizing I missed a step. I throw the bathing suit in my hands behind me and follow his lead, jumping into bed.

A little while later, the ocean shimmers against the bright sun. My body melts into a yellow cushion on the lounge chair as my right leg dangles down and my toes wiggle in the sand. Eric's fingers intertwine with mine, his loud snores causing me to giggle. A large palm tree sways, its verdant leaves offering a refreshing shelter from the heat.

Once, when I was eight, mom smiled while getting me dressed. I couldn't close the large gold buttons gracing my checkered herringbone skirt suit. She had bought me new Mary Janes for this occasion, shiny black patent-leather with a little bow by the toes. Mom curled my hair and placed it half up in a rhinestone clip. My birdlike legs straggled from beneath the pencil skirt. The sleeves of my blazer hung slightly over my palms. It felt like playing dress-up for the day, being a grown-up to join Dad at work. It was a new job at a company called Fimat.

Dad and I took the Long Island Railroad to Penn Station and from there the subway downtown. Red graffiti was sprayed across the silver metal doors of the train. I remember being scared of the grungy atmosphere and unpredictable people. The walls of the tunnel whirled by as the train sped along the tracks. My body jiggled back and forth on the orange seat, holding his hand tight.

The rush of people running past us was intimidating, but his arm held my waist as we climbed the flights of stairs toward the street. Dark business suits, all moving robotically on the pavement, appeared like something out of a movie. Everyone walked with intense purpose. My dad stopped, tapping my shoulder. I looked up at his face and he seemed larger than life. His tall body was outlined by the narrow Towers behind him. His knees bent, coming down to my eye level. He held my body close and pointed to the buildings in front of us. "This is where I work. It's called the Twin Towers. Neat, huh?"

I arched my head back, taking in the immense scale of the

buildings. All I could do was stare in awe, trying to understand how something so big could be on this earth. The black rows of windows that stacked upward into the clouds seemed to reach heaven.

My dad's palm on the center of my back guided me into the revolving doors. His hands felt soft and warm against the fabric of my suit. We weaved in and out of line, scurrying toward a large open room. The shiny marble floors beneath my shoes stretched endlessly, leading to a never-ending grand staircase. The coliseum-like structure was capped by a sphere-shaped glass ceiling. Gigantic palm trees, taller than the ones I see now in the Dominican Republic, were scattered at the bottom of the steps, complementing the immense size of the room. Their brown and yellow stalks burst out of the lobby, spiraling toward the sky with abundant leaves of green grazing the transparent roof.

I yanked my dad's hand, getting his attention. "Daddy, what is this place?"

He pointed in the air to the large green leaves. "This is the Winter Garden atrium. See the ceiling? It's ten stories high, a glass-vaulted pavilion. These palm trees are the only ones in New York, and they're in the lobby of my building."

It was the most beautiful thing I'd ever seen, like being transported to an exotic beach. One would never know we were at the tip of Manhattan.

My memories of that day scatter to snippets. I remember running around my dad's office and some man yelling out, "I hate kids." My dad and I both laughed at the employee's frustration, and I continued playing hide-and-seek among the box-like structures of cubicles. Dad's secretary gave me a large plastic toy rat. I have no idea where she found it, but it was the ugliest thing I'd ever seen, with big white teeth and a long curvy tail. I'd place it on all the employees' chairs, hide in corners, and burst out in laughter when they'd approach their desk to find the disgusting rodent. My dad, in and out of meetings, would play with me when he could, momentarily transforming into a child himself. His secretary took out a small metal box filled with more money than I'd ever seen in my life. She taught me about petty cash and explained that my dad was in charge of signing paychecks and making sure people did their jobs and got paid. I nodded. "Oh, so he's kind of like Scrooge?"

She laughed. "Yes, but a nice Scrooge."

Suddenly, Eric's fingers stroke the top of my arm. "Ash, are you okay?"

I find myself still staring at the swaying leaves of the palm tree. I give a reassuring smile. "Yeah, sorry. I was just reminded of my dad." I can't bring myself to say more.

Eric takes a long sip of an icy cocktail with a pineapple perched on the rim of the glass. "Ash, I'd really like to visit the memorial with you. I know the museum's opening soon. We can do it to-gether. It'll be hard, but I'd like to be there for you when you see it for the first time."

The answer is easy. In a situation where my heart is on the line, it's a no-brainer. I sit up and kiss his cheek. "I can only go to Ground Zero with family. I know you'd be a great support for me there, but I'm not comfortable with that yet. Honestly, I don't think I'll be ready to bring anyone there until I'm married. The man who stands by my side in that museum, that has to be my husband. It'll be like meeting my dad for the first time. Getting to know my father, about his life, the work he did, and his legacy. Worst of all, the way he died. I can't share that with anyone other than family."

My body trembles. Have I offended him in some way? But all I know how to do is protect my heart, to prepare myself for tra-gedy or bad news. If I expect the worst, then I'll never be caught off guard. The same goes for men. Eric's been wonderful, but his feelings for me can change at a moment's notice. What if I bring him downtown to the memorial with my family? He would be part of our world that day. A place in which we cry, reflect, and express the most vulnerable sides of ourselves. If Eric and I were to break up, I'd have exposed myself and my family to a person no longer in our inner circle. Someone who was with us on the most sacred of days and now no longer a part of our lives. I can't allow that to happen.

Eric stands. His hands wipe the sand from his bathing suit as it trickles onto his chair. He climbs behind me, sitting down, and

I lean back into his chest. The gentle sound of the tide turning plays like a melody, soothing my mind. I take the towel by my feet, pulling it over my body, and close my eyes. My weight shifts entirely onto him, giving into relaxation. I can feel his fingers combing through my hair, and I begin to drift off.

He whispers in my ear, "I already know your dad, he's very much a part of you. But we will visit the museum together, when you're ready. And I can promise you this, I'll be that man standing beside you when you go."

16

The Things I Never Told You

My mom and I sit on a stiff wooden bench, which is irritating my back. Or is it just this place that makes me uncomfortable? The dreary funeral home on the south shore of Long Island brings goosebumps to my arms. It's hard to figure out if I have the chills from the casket that rests a few feet ahead of me or from the sea of people in dark suits, all weeping. I hold my mom's hand, appreciating the soft feel of her skin. My other hand rests near my mouth as my teeth gnaw at the skin by my fingernails.

When I got the phone call that Jill's dad had suddenly died of a heart attack, I wish I could say that I fell to the ground in tears. But it wasn't the first time I'd received news of a close friend having lost someone they love. Every time, my body reacts the same. I become numb and a shadow comes over me, possibly as a protective layer: my subconscious not allowing myself to go to a dark place. Haven't I mourned enough? If I continue to do so for every person who loses someone, how will I ever be happy?

I don't feel that everyone in my life mourned for me when it was my turn. Sure, during the first few months after 9/11 I had crowds of visitors and an inundation of phone calls. But eventually, the world kept turning. People continued on with their lives, joyful and happy. The days turned to nights and the seasons changed. Everyone evolved while I was stuck in grief. No one else can be counted on to get out of that funk. It has to happen on your own when you're mentally ready to dust yourself off and pick up the pieces. Does this make me bitter? Am I unsympathetic to those who experience loss now? It's possible, but it's also who I've become, and I can't change it.

The rows of filled benches surrounded by pastel flowers and stained-glass windows remind me of my dad's memorial service. It was an unusual circumstance, a week after he was killed. His body hadn't been recovered, making a traditional funeral and burial impossible. Somehow, though, my mom wanted that memorial as a way, I suppose, to bring some kind of closure to the situation. A place where people could pay their respects and then allow our family to try and move on, even though my dad would always be considered not dead, but missing, in every police file from now until the end of time.

As Jill stands on the platform in front of the large crowd, she offers a eulogy to her father. How did I do the same at sixteen years old? My mom and brother were too distraught, but someone in the family had to speak. I remember walking up to the bema, patting down my pinstriped black skirt. Any feelings I had, I bottled up. I took a deep breath, looked at the crowd of people filling the seats, halls, and rafters, and began. It was easy for me that day to express how I felt. I think I needed for the people in the room to remember why they were there. It wasn't for 9/11 or the thousands of lives lost. On that day, in that particular moment, it was about my dad. He deserved to be remembered solely for the selfless and unique person that he was.

Jill is remarkably poised and collected in front of the crowd. A baggy tailored shirt is tucked into her trousers. It belonged to her father, and Jill wears it to remember him. While she speaks, I wonder what's going through her mind. Are these the words she really wants to say to her dad, or the things she needs for him to hear?

Once a year, I have an incredibly vivid dream. It's always the same and goes way too quickly. My dad and I are walking on a beach together. His skin is bronzed and healthy, his eyes are fiercely blue. We stroll side by side, never touching, knowing that we're in two different worlds. I'll tell him about my life, and he listens quietly, taking in my words and the sound of my voice. As our feet imprint the sand, each step is a reminder that our time is limited. Like an hourglass running, we know at any minute we'll be taken away from each other. My dad will cut me off mid-sentence and say, "Time's up, I have to go." I always wake in a pool of sweat, panting in fright from the realness. What would I say to him now? I would tell him all the random little events that have significance to me but maybe not to someone else:

It's a dream of mine to get married one day. I wish you could be here to dance with me to "Butterfly Kisses," just like we did at my bat mitzvah.

I know I was lucky to have you for as long as I did. You were a present father, and the time that we had together fulfills me.

I once told you I hate you. We were in the elevator at Indiana University when we were visiting Josh at college. You were pretending it was going to get stuck, and I was annoyed and scared. I said those three words and instantly regretted it. You became quiet, and I wonder, did I make you cry? I still feel terrible about it.

Did I ever thank you for working so hard to try and give me everything I ever wanted? I know I said thank you after family dinners and for birthday presents. But on those random days, just a thank you for being you, for commuting more than four hours a day to provide for your family.

In elementary school I would watch as school plays went on or a student's birthday came and their dads would be there videotaping. Usually, you weren't there. I knew you were at work and I was never resentful. I was grateful to have a dad who cared so much about me to work as hard as he did.

We traveled all around the world: Italy, France, the Bahamas, Aruba, Arizona. The memories were incredible, and yet some of my favorite moments with you were the simple ones. When you used to come into my room, crawl under the covers with me, and pretend the boogeyman was coming. When we would sit on the black leather couch in the den as you watched football on Sundays with a soda and pretzel rods on the table. I would sit next to you and we would put our hands on top of one another—yours first, then mine, then yours, as they went higher and higher into the air.

I loved watching you. Whether you were using the grill to make BBQ or checking the chemistry of the pool to make sure the right amounts of chemicals were in it. Or when you'd sit in the office as you did taxes or worked on the computer, you left your imprint on each and every room.

You and Mom threw me a surprise birthday party when I turned fifteen. It was at an Italian restaurant with all of my friends. You were standing in the back and yelled out "Happy Birthday" as I walked inside. I know how hard it was for you to leave work early that day to be there for me.

As the eulogies for Jill's dad continue, I blink, my eyes burning as I attempt to keep in the tears. My mom's finger rubs my cheek, wiping the wet skin. I hate crying, knowing how much it hurts her. In an attempt to brighten my mood, she tries to distract me. "Umm, Ash? What's with your outfit?"

I look down at my black Nike sneakers and the loose black trousers around my waist. My mom's fit and flare dress hugs her curves, her black blazer with silver buttons accentuating her bustline and providing some style. She looks polished and put together.

"What?" I whisper back. "I don't have funeral clothes. All my heels are for dates, way too high. Same with my black dresses, all with a low neckline or backless, not exactly appropriate. But who's really looking at what I wear to a funeral anyway?"

She shakes her head as if she's raised me better. "Ash, think about it. When you're at a funeral you know everyone. You're in the same circle, connected to the person you lost. Yes, it's a sad day, but your outfit doesn't need to reflect that. Look around!"

I ignore her silly remarks. Funerals aren't fashion shows. I scan the rows of people; mostly women surround me. They all have long legs fit with black tights leading to slim figures in tight dresses. The men interspersed are all in perfectly fitting suits. Maybe she has a point.

She pats my arm. "Remind me to take you shopping tomorrow for a proper black dress and pumps. Keep it in the back of your closet, then when you need it, *bam*! It's there. Everyone has a funeral dress."

Suddenly, in this solemn room, I can't help but giggle. How does she do it? Get my mind off of death for a few minutes?

She kisses my cheek. "Promise me this. One day, hopefully far from now, when I'm not here, you'll be in a beautiful dress. Maybe get your hair and nails done, too. It couldn't hurt."

I smile, looking down so no one can see. Sadly, I know she's dead serious.

I turn toward my mom, whispering, "Remember when we sat Shiva for Dad? What Dad's best friend had to do?"

She covers her lips with her manicured fingers. I can tell by the shaking of her shoulders that she's giggling. "I'll never forget. Too many people showed up at our house, for days on end. We couldn't fit them all! Not to mention they'd knock on the door at the oddest hours, eight in the morning, eleven at night. Even if we told people set times, they didn't listen."

I chime in, my mouth close to her ear. "So Tom sat in his car in our driveway for days. He had a cup of coffee in his hand and read the newspaper. Anyone who pulled up to the house, he'd turn away. I think he actually enjoyed sitting post like that."

She quietly laughed and nodded. "Your dad would have gotten such a kick out of it." Her arm wraps around my back. "I'm glad we can laugh about it now. Thank god."

My head falls on her shoulder as we continue listening to the eulogies. In a moment when we should feel intense sadness, we are okay. We're grateful to have each other. The world really does go on. There are no rules, set in black and white, when it comes to death. One person's saddest day may not be so for the individual sitting next to them. For the first time in my life, I accept that and realize it's okay.

17

The Memorial

My body squeezes between the members of the crowd at the sharp corner of the 9/11 memorial fountain. The tight space where my dad's name is engraved in stone is in a prominent location. The etched letters are just feet away and directly facing the entryway to the 9/11 museum. My heart thumps, waiting for the large doors of the oddly shaped glass-and-metal building to open. Its boxlike exterior seems small compared to the breadth of space I anticipate being inside. Sweat seeps through my black blouse and I nervously pat down the fabric, hoping the moisture will dissolve. What does someone wear to an event like this anyway? It feels like a funeral, or an unveiling of sorts. Crowds of people outline the fountain, rows of bodies along the border. It's now May 15, 2014, the first time the museum is open to the families of the victims, and, just for today, we're the only ones allowed inside.

I'm sandwiched between my mom and brother as we stare down

the fountain. The trickling sound of water soothes my nerves. My brother lightly nudges my arm. "You haven't said a word since we got here. I know you don't like coming to these events, but there really wasn't another option. Today is the only day we can visit in peace. After this, it's with tourists and the rest of the world."

My teeth grind against each other, taking a moment to respond. "I hate being told when I have to do something and how I have to do it. It's bad enough that we have to share this day with hundreds of people. I just want to go home."

I breathe in the fresh air, holding it in my lungs until I feel I will burst, then slowly exhale. I close my eyes, hoping the long breaths keep in the tears. "I'm scared to see what's down there. I don't want to see how Daddy was hurt or details about what happened to him." The bitter taste of my lunch sits in my throat, and I look around for a trash can, sure that my stomach can't take the anticipation.

Josh's arms stretch around Rachel's tiny frame as he embraces her. She gently takes my hand in hers, holding tight. She squeezes my fingers, a sincere gesture to show that I'm thought of. I suddenly crave a partner of my own. Someone who can hold me and remind me that I'm okay now. Eric's sincere smile comes to my mind. I imagine his firm hands around my back. I pretend to hear his strong voice whisper in my ear. He's the reminder I need right now, that I'm in a happy place. That this nightmare of my past is over and I've rebuilt a better life.

Mom taps me on the shoulder, handing me a ticket. "Let's go, they've started letting people in." She wraps her arm around my shoulder as Joe walks by her side, his hand around her waist. My eyes travel between my mom and brother, each with the people they love. The pain in my chest reflects a hint of jealousy. My family is able to bring their significant others to this place. Easily opening up their innermost fears with the ones they love. How come I'm not able to do the same? Ironic how I don't want to go into this museum and face my past, even though I feel stuck in it.

Mom and Josh walk hand in hand. I follow quickly, like a baby duckling afraid to be left behind. Upon entering, I'm overwhelmed by the tall concrete walls that lead upward to the ceiling. The space is extraordinarily large and the crowds of people that had stood in line to get in now seem like small ants scurrying through the tunnels of this place. Gripping the metal banister, I descend the long flight of stairs. They bend and turn, leading to another maze-like spiral that travels deeper into the ground. One foot in front of the other, I try not to fall, my senses distorted. My palm rubs my chest, feeling the beating of my heart.

The stark white museum and open space should feel unfamiliar and barren. I'm surprised, though, by how at home I feel, knowing this is the closest I'll ever be to my dad. The silence is astonishing—I swear I could hear a pin drop if I had one. There's no chatter or sound of footsteps against the floor.

I arrive at the bottom level and follow my family toward a wide wall covered with a sea of faces. The photographs of victims lost have been knitted onto a tapestry that now hangs several feet above my head. The eyes of the deceased, thousands of them, stare from the quilt, and I scan the faces in search of my dad. Joe stands next to my mom, caressing her lower back as she, too, searches. I wonder how she must feel, missing and remembering her husband while her partner stands beside her. She hasn't cried, far from it actually. With her calm demeanor and perfectly planned footsteps, she's a leader unlike one I've ever seen. She guides our emotions and our movements, knowing that if she can keep it together, we can, too.

My brother steps close to the tapestry and points above his head. "Look! It's Dad."

We all move closer to the wall as my brother's hand remains raised in the air. His finger almost touches the smooth thread that creates the image of my father's porcelain skin. Suddenly, a man approaches, tapping Josh on the shoulder. "Excuse me, sir. I apologize, but you can't touch the art. Please step back."

The security guard's wide eyes and hunched shoulders reveal his embarrassment. He doesn't want to have to be the one to tell us that we can't touch my father's face. We all nod in silence, migrating backward while keeping eye contact with the image of my father. Just like reality, we have his photographs and the memories, but there's nothing tangible about him anymore. I close my eyes, imagining his cheek rubbing against mine. On the weekends, he wouldn't shave his beard. Sunday mornings, he would rub the course grainy hairs on his face against my smooth skin and I would laugh as it tickled my nose down to my chin. Even if I could touch the artifact in front of me, I'd never get back that feeling.

My mom turns her back to the wall and begins walking away. Like a game of follow-the-leader, we trace her footsteps into an adjacent area where a firetruck is parked in the middle of a room. I take in its tremendous size: how in the world did this get down here? The gray marks of dust are a reminder of the heroes lost, the firefighters and police officers. It's impossible to imagine having the bravery to go into the Towers, knowing you might not ever get out. My face feels warm, and I take deep breaths. I will not cry in front of all these people, next to my family—I can't be so vulnerable out in the open. I turn quickly, ready to see something different that doesn't bring tears to my eyes.

To my right is a steel antenna, its spirals twisting and turning around rusted rods. It looks foreign, like part of a spaceship. Originally 360 feet long, this was at the top of Tower 1, my dad's building. Its size still seems massive, but I cringe thinking about the remainders. Where did the rest of this piece go? How did this gigantic structure fall from over a thousand feet in the air and still remain somewhat intact? To think, this thing, this oddly shaped metal, was closer to my father when he was killed than I was. My back tingles and I cringe, frightened of the image of being so high in the air and then to have fallen. My heart sinks into my chest and I look up at the ceiling in an attempt to distract my mind. I clench my fists tight, squeezing. I have to be strong. I can't break in front of my family.

A white wall holds large images of the hijackers. Nineteen faces all with empty, dark eyes pop out and catch my attention. I point to one of their photographs, leaning in toward my mother. "How disgusting! The terrorists are immortalized here? It's not right, it's not fair that they should be remembered. That's exactly what they wanted."

She shrugs her shoulders, contemplating the question. "I don't know, Ash. This is what evil looks like. These men and their brutality, the harm they caused to so many people. Maybe if we have these pictures and know what horror looks like, it helps us to learn."

I shake my head in disapproval. The sight of the terrorists turns my stomach, and I feel nauseous. The temperature seems to have risen, and my body is warm with fury. This isn't what my dad would have wanted. I roll my eyes, walking away not nearly quick enough, swearing I'll never allow myself to see this display again.

In a nearby exhibit, rooms lead from one space to the next, filled with collected pieces that were saved from the day the Towers were hit. The artifacts sit behind glass casings, protected and safe. Clothing ripped in pieces and covered with dirt hangs as a symbol of people who escaped, the cloth on their backs proof of what they'd outrun.

My brother touches a casing that holds a metal sculpture. "Ash, this was in the Cantor Fitzgerald office." It's now tarnished, and its distorted appearance leaves much to the imagination. "It was beautiful, back then. It's incredible to think that this was found in all of that rubble."

I think of my dad, in a hurry to catch a meeting or to take an important phone call. Did he walk by this every day? I remember his busy schedule, sometimes unavailable if I called to say hi. I'd leave voicemails with his secretary. "Please tell my dad I got one hundred percent on my Earth science test. The one he helped me to study for all week." She'd give a sweet giggle and respond, "I'll be sure to let him know."

Flat screens on the walls play video footage, a timeline of 9/11. I can't bear to watch as the planes fly into the buildings and people in the streets run. Each hour of that day is portrayed here. With every footstep, the nightmare becomes real again. The Towers collapse, monstrous clouds of dust rise into the air. I shiver, not wanting to see any more.

I walk forward toward an exhibit. It's similar to the tapestry, except this time it's photographs. A multitude of ethnicities, ages, and genders of the victims create endless rows of color along a dark wall. I spot my dad instantly; he's surrounded by so many people that look to be in their twenties and early thirties. Some of the women were pregnant, all killed. The horror of that day did not discriminate. It didn't matter if you were a man or woman or how much life the person still had left to live. No one was pardoned.

Now I realize where I am, in the room where the recordings are curated. The dark space is filled with flat screens and headphones. The argument that I had with my family years before comes back to me, along with my refusal to put pictures of myself in here or record memories that I had with my dad.

I approach a bright screen and begin typing in my last name. In a few moments, JEFFREY GOLDFLAM, in bold black letters, lights up the prompter. My right hand quickly taps, and I lift a set of bulky headphones. A faint whisper comes through the speaker and my finger taps the monitor, increasing the volume until my mother's voice becomes crystal clear.

Her soft tone effortlessly radiates into my ear. "Jeff and I met in high school. He was my true love." As her story unfolds, pictures of my parents flash across the screen. The bright light illuminates my face in the dim room. I've seen this picture before. My father stands next to my mom—he has brown hair reaching his shoulders and plaid pants on. My mother is wearing a blue tie-dyed shirt that wrinkles as her arms cross her chest, protecting from the cold snow in the background.

My mind wanders, remembering sitting on Dad's lap when I was a little girl. He hugged me tight, his arms wrapping around my belly, holding this photograph in front of my eyes, its edges bruised and yellow, reflecting the wear and tear of time. He pointed to the rickety old porch where my parents held each other in the photo. "See, that's Binghamton, where your mom came to visit me in college. One day, you'll be in college, too. No boyfriends allowed, though."

I'd laugh and say, "But Daddy, when will I be old enough for a boyfriend?"

With a stern look on his face, he'd whisper in my ear, "Never." Then, with the slightest tilt, the side of his mouth would curve up, revealing that Mona Lisa smile, the truth resting behind his light grin.

I clench my throat, holding back the tears, yet they begin to drip down my cheeks.

Another picture flashes by, and I hold my breath, bending closer. It was taken on the back deck of my house. My dad wears a white T-shirt and black aviator glasses. He holds me tight, my small arms wrapped around his neck while my loose curls flow across my face. My big smile reveals little gaps where new teeth are yet to come in. It's as if I can still hear the Madonna ballads playing. My dad had struggled that morning to carry the Yamaha speakers outside for a family barbecue. His large hands held mine as he led me through a series of twirls, the trees blurry as I spun.

A burning in my heart grows as guilt rushes through my veins, traveling throughout my body. I can taste the salty tears which pass my mouth, creating a puddle of moisture on the screen, blurring the pictures below. It was a simple day, but it has now become a cherished memory. I close my eyes, pressing my lids tightly, wishing I could transport myself back to that moment in my backyard.

Then I gasp, catching my breath like I've emerged from a turbulent sea, almost drowning. I get it now, why there have to be pictures of me in the museum. I'm able to gain back a memory with my dad that would have otherwise been gone forever. This museum is about who Dad was—it reflects his life and his children, the memories that were dear to him. Captured in this slideshow spinning before my eyes, a photo reel brings my past back to me in the present. This place is proof that my dad lives on. Through the eyes of me, my family, and the rest of the world, he won't be forgotten. This is about my relationship with my father and our memories of him—our story is not just about the way he was killed.

I press my palm against the monitor where a picture of Dad's face is displayed. It's as if he's here, standing next to me, telling me that it's okay to think of him, acknowledge his memorial, and most of all, move forward with my life. I whisper ever so delicately, "I hear you, Daddy, and I love you."

I set the headphones aside and am startled that Mom is standing next to me. I press my lips against her cheek. "Thank you for including pictures of Daddy and me in the slideshow. You were right, I'm happy they're in here. The world needs to know what an incredible dad he was."

She stands in silence, relief sweeping across her face as her jawline loosens. "I did what I thought was best. I had a feeling that one day you'd change your mind. There's no rulebook for this, Ash. No directions on how to be a parent when your child loses their dad this way. These are impossible decisions I have to make. I'm trying, I've tried . . ."

"Don't explain yourself. I'm saying I'm grateful for what you've done."

My fingers intertwine with hers as we exit the room. I can see Josh, Rachel, and Joe huddled in the hallway, chatting. As we stand in a circle, I take inventory of our group. With every movement, they appear in slow motion. Like wounded soldiers home from battle, we're emotionally exhausted. My reflection in a dark window stares back at me. My skin is a drop paler from when I entered the building hours before. My eyes are swollen and red.

Mom breaks the silence, holding up her hands. "This has been an overwhelming day. It's too much to take in at once, and I think we've had enough."

We turn our heads as if lost, taking in our surroundings one last time. All of our eyes meet, a non-verbal, unanimous decision that we've seen all that we can handle for now. I nod in agreement. My chest and shoulders suddenly feel lighter, knowing that nothing more is coming my way, for today anyway. My heart aches, but now I'm full of peace. I got what I didn't even know I needed by coming here. My eyes dart around the building. I climb the flights upward and begin to see the twilight sky. With every glimpse of the outside peeking through the windows, the air in the room is easier to take in and I can breathe again.

Mom looks at her watch. "It's five p.m. I made a reservation at a restaurant a few blocks away for five thirty. Ash, you told Eric to meet us there?"

My body begins to refuel as I think of Eric's presence. "Yeah, it was best he didn't come to this. But I thought having him at dinner would be nice."

We enter Les Halles, a cozy French restaurant where we are pointed in the direction of a large circular table. I take a moment and let my fingers comb through my hair. I open up my purse and apply a layer of fresh nude lipstick. I don't want to look like a complete mess after all the crying. As my heels tap against the checkered black-and-white floor of the brasserie, Eric walks through the door just in time.

I hesitate for a moment. How will he react in this situation? As my family picks seats around the table, they smile and kiss him hello, attempting to nurture a happier mood. I watch as Eric gracefully travels from seat to seat, hugging each family member. His brown sports coat embraces his broad shoulders, and he looks the part of a successful businessman, someone who has it together. He handles the delicate situation with such ease. My heart skips a beat, amazed with his poise. He doesn't give the usual "How are you?" with a head tilt to the side in sympathy. No sad look on his face attempting to be in our shoes. He's simply himself, and I know I've found a truly unique and special person. Eric's fingers trace the outline of my knee under the table. He talks effortlessly with everyone, but it's clear that his mind is on me. The touch of his skin against mine says it all. How is it that he so easily fits into this puzzle which is my family? Like a missing piece found way too late, he complements us.

We pick up the menus and discuss appetizers and entrees. I laugh as Eric and my brother go head-to-head, placing orders for oysters and steak tartar. They jokingly banter over Manhattan's best steaks and where to get the freshest seafood. Trickles of red wine flow from bottles as servers fill our glasses to the brim and we compare orders. My mom laughs as I shake my head, rejecting all the salivating mouths that want a bite of the steaming French onion soup in front of me.

My mom raises her glass. "A toast, to our resilient family. I couldn't be prouder of the people that we've become."

She pauses for a moment. We all look around, a bit saddened, knowing that such an integral member of our family isn't here.

Then she looks at Josh and me. "Daddy would be so thrilled with the adults you've become, with the life choices you've made." She turns toward my sister-in-law and then to Eric. She continues, "Thank you, too, for making my children so happy and for completing our family. It's not easy to understand our situation, and you both do so flawlessly, and I thank you."

Our glasses chime together, each clink a celebration of life. My mom tells stories of our childhoods, of Josh as a rebellious teenager and me as a little girl obsessed with Barbies. We laugh so hard that we cry. At one moment the tables around us throw looks of annoyance, displeased with our loudness and outpouring of laughter. But we don't care. We sit united as a family, together and happy.

18

The Turquoise Ring

A fifteen-foot Polynesian statue towers over me. The tiki structure depicts a sculpted face, the eyes, nose, and mouth in odd shapes and sizes. Eric's hands sweep across the piece, painted gold in an attempt to fit in with the chic vibe at the Montauk Beach Club Hotel. We step aside every few minutes as tourists walk by and ask to take a picture in front of the gigantic statue.

Eric squints, gazing at the top of the artwork, where vacationers exit their rooms in straw hats and sheer caftans covering bikinis. "It wasn't always like this?" The perplexed look on his face is a sign that he still doesn't understand how 1960s' kitsch fits into the bohemian aesthetic that now dominates the East End.

I stare at the structure, and even though its color is different, I still see it how I did as a little girl—when its eyes were royal blue and the lips painted blood red. "At night the inside of the mouth lights up really bright, it's so creepy. At least, that's what used to happen, when I stayed here years ago."

He shrugs his shoulders. "What was this place called back in the day?"

I laugh. "The Ronjo. It was disgusting! My parents booked a hotel out here but somehow the reservation fell through. There was nowhere else to stay so for one night we had to check in at the only motel available, and this was it."

At the time, my parents were completely grossed out. They couldn't wait to leave. But ever since we stayed here, we'd always talk about our night at *The Ronjjoooo*, as my dad would call it, joking around as he accentuated the letters in the name.

A lady taps my shoulder and I turn. She's attractive, in her early forties. Her long brown curls flow across her face from the ocean breeze. She has a soft voice and holds out her iPhone in my direction. *"Puedes tomar una foto?"*

My mind is stuck, unable to translate. It's not the language that's throwing me off, but her hand that holds the cell phone. I stare at her fingers wrapped around the plastic; one in particular displays a sterling silver ring. The tiny piece of jewelry has a round turquoise stone at the center, surrounded by three black lines etched into the metal. I've seen this ring once before, and up until now, I thought it was one of a kind.

Eric notices the stillness in my body. He calls my name loudly, attempting to regain my attention. "Ash, she wants you to take a photo for her."

He shakes his head, waiting for me to take action. After several seconds, his arm extends outward, gesturing for the woman to walk toward the statue and pose. I watch as she smiles, resting her body against the warm stone.

Her hands move along the curves of the chiseled face. But as if there is a fog surrounding her, all that remains clear to me is her delicate finger as it glides across the structure, the silver ring glinting in the sun.

She smiles at Eric and presses her palms together in a way that looks like she's about to pray. *"Gracias."*

Where did she buy this piece of jewelry? Does she know how special it is?

I point to her finger. "Where did you get that? The ring on your hand?"

She shakes her head and a pit forms in my stomach, remembering that there's no way to communicate. Her hand waves in the air in appreciation and then she walks away toward the quaint town.

Eric's arm wraps around my shoulder. "Ash, what is it that you wanted to tell her?"

I exhale, as if returning to reality. "It's a long story."

His wrist meets his eyes, and he grabs my hand. "C'mon, we have a seven o'clock dinner reservation, and I don't want to be late."

I laugh. "How is it that I planned this vacation, an escape from the city in the heat of the summer, yet you were still able to sneak something into the itinerary?"

His quick strides leave me out of breath as I attempt to keep up. "I only made one plan and that was for tonight. The reviews of Scarpetta have been awesome, and I really want to check it out."

"That's the new restaurant inside the hotel at Gurney's, right? Did you know that it overlooks the beach? It's supposed to be beautiful."

Eric's eyes widen. "Sounds amazing. All I know about is the food."

I pat his stomach, the skin just a bit softer than when we met almost two years ago. Eric's love of trying new cuisines and restaurants has us eating all throughout Manhattan on a regular basis. "Don't be too bad an influence on me," I tease. "It's bathing suit season."

He throws a mischievous smile in my direction. "I know a way we can burn off the calories, don't worry about it." We giggle like naughty teenagers.

That evening, Eric and I sit at a table perched high on a hill, overlooking the ocean. If it weren't for the view, one would think we were in Manhattan. Obscure light fixtures molded into modern shapes hang from the ceiling. The wooden gray chevron floor expands along a flat room with sleek white couches and winged-back chairs. Our table sits on a balcony, a small candle in between us illuminating the outdoor area. Droplets of moisture accumulate on my arms, the ocean mist floating upward.

Eric's spoon dives into the chocolate cake in front of us and he closes his eyes as he chews the dessert, savoring every bite. He pushes his chair back, patting his belly. "Would it be too much if we asked for the stromboli from the bread basket to take home?"

I put my hands over my face, slightly mortified. "Babe, please don't ask the waiter for a to-go bag of bread."

Eric's smile fills the room, and I'm immediately reminded of our first date and my attraction to him. He holds up his hands in defeat. "I'm only kidding! We can always come back tomorrow and have the same dinner all over again."

He winks, knowing his jokes have gone over my head. I always take him too seriously. He turns, takes the sports coat from his chair, and passes it across the table. "Put this on, it gets chilly here at night, so close to the water."

The beige-and-navy-checkered fabric does nothing to complement the maxi dress I'm wearing, which shows just the right amount of skin. But I gratefully grab the jacket and throw it over my shoulders. The sudden relief from the cool breeze warms my body. I drop my fork onto the white dessert plate. "Well, I'm full for the rest of the vacation. This was absolutely delicious."

Eric stands up and gestures toward the ocean. "Let's head out there, walk off some of this food."

Our hands intertwine as he leads me down flights of stairs to the water. With every step, the air becomes thick with salty vapor. The sky has turned dark, and only the twinkling lights from the restaurant above guide us. I grasp Eric's arm, the winding turns causing me to question my choice of shoes for the evening.

The beach is empty this time of night. Just one bonfire lights the sand ahead. "Look! How beautiful is that?" I point to the bright red flames.

Eric turns, heading in that direction.

I pull his arm. "No, this looks like it's reserved for someone. I don't want to get in trouble, see?" A green gingham blanket lies a few feet from the fire. On top of it, a bottle of wine peeks out of a bucket.

We approach the lavish setup, and Eric's eyes look up and down, observing the contents on the blanket. "They even have a s'mores kit—impressive." He nods in approval.

I look around, waiting to be kicked out of the area by the people this awaits.

Eric smiles. "This is for us. Thanks for planning a weekend get-away. But you know me better than to just sit back and let you handle all the details. I had to throw in a little something of my own." He kneels down, opens the bottle of sparkling rosé, and pours two generous glasses.

My jaw drops, my mind scrambling to find the right words.

Eric sits on the blanket and pats the ground beside him, gestur-ing for me to join. I oblige, take the cold crystal glass from his hand, and sip the sweet wine. Speckles of moonlight reflect off the ocean, and the water sparkles as its ripples shimmer toward the land.

The warmth of the fire spreads throughout my body. I relax, my toes playing in the sand along the blanket. "You know, my dad used to take me to this beach when I was a kid. It wasn't super fancy then, just a casual spot to play in the waves."

Eric holds a thin wooden stick, gently placing a marshmallow on the far end. I watch as the flames take over, browning the fluffy white puff until it's soft. He takes two graham crackers, sand-wiching the charcoaled dessert, then points it in my direction. I lean forward, taking a bite as crumbs fall into my lap.

Eric laughs, his finger rubbing the sticky mess from the side of my mouth. "I know all about your time with your dad in Mon-tauk. How you played in the ocean with him when you were little. This place is special for us now, too. It's where I've come with you, and we've made new memories together."

I cuddle closer to him. "Being in Montauk as an adult, with you—it's been a dream."

A wave crashes several feet away, the mist spraying in the air between us. "That's what I was going to say next. Ashley, you mean the world to me."

I kiss his lips. "I love you so much."

He puts his hands on my shoulders and looks into my eyes. "Ash, please stop interrupting me."

Our shoulders shake as we begin to laugh. I place my right hand over my mouth, my words now muffled. "I'm so sorry!"

Eric reaches into his pocket and pulls out a black velvet box, opening it quickly before my eyes. "Ashley, I'll love you for the rest of my life. Will you marry me?"

My heart pants wildly, and I jump up and down. "Oh my gosh! I mean yes! Yes, I'll marry you!"

My hands hold Eric's cheeks as we kiss. My body is in shock, and I swear I'd forget where I was if it weren't for the warm crackling of the fire beside us. Our arms wrap around one another, and we lie on the blanket, looking up at the stars.

I stare in awe at the princess-cut stone. "Should we call our parents? Tell them the news?"

His brown eyes meet mine and I know he's thinking the same thing I am. "Let's wait a little longer. Take in this moment. Let it be ours, just you and me."

We rush back to our room and find ourselves in bed. Eric's head rests on my chest, the fine strands of his hair tickling my face. The heavy sound of his breathing is a sign that he's asleep. I wish I could do the same, but my body shivers with nerves, the excitement from the evening not yet worn off.

I tighten my muscles to control the shaking, trying not to wake him. The light from the moon shines through the open window. Its round shape illuminates the white sheets that encase our bodies. I close my eyes, imagining the waves crashing down on the sand just feet away from our hotel room. I hold my hand close to my face. The stones on the band of the engagement ring sparkle, even with the lights out. I've never worn much jewelry on my hands or fingers. It has always felt confining to me, like handcuffs. But for this ring, I'm happy to make an exception. There is only one other ring I have ever felt this way about, but it was lost. My head sinks deeply into the fluffy goose down pillow, and I close my eyes, remembering a family vacation from when I was a little girl.

Layers of mahogany and browns swept across the jagged surface of the mountain range outside of Scottsdale, Arizona. It looked as if a paint brush had just floated across the rock, creating intricate texture and detail. The Jeep Wrangler we were riding in took steep turns along the narrow pathways, and my body jolted from side to side. I was cuddled next to Dad, his arms wrapped around me in an effort to keep me warm.

"Daddy, didn't we come on this vacation for pool weather?"

He pointed to the top of the mountain; the peaks protruding toward the sky were blanketed in white frost. "Baby girl, this is the first time it's snowed here in decades. This weather was not planned for."

I rolled my eyes. "Dad! I told you not to call me that anymore. I'm going to be ten. I'm too old for 'baby girl.'"

My mom sat up front beside the driver, turning her head to listen in. "Well, I think our little off-road excursion to the Native American reservation is going to end fairly soon if we don't get some warm clothes on our backs."

The tour guide behind the wheel smiled, his tan skin gathering in wrinkles. "My tribe lives a few miles down the road. There's a store that sells some sweatshirts and clothing. We should be there in a few minutes."

Soon enough, the tires on the car screeched to a halt. Light poured through the glass windows of a small wooden cabin a few feet ahead. The brick chimney belched black smoke into the sky, and I could imagine the heat inside wiping my goosebumps away.

I followed my parents into the small store toward a wall of wooden cubbies filled with hoodies and sweats with Arizona logos. A strong scent of burning wood filled the room, and the fireplace crackled. Zigzag patterns along the hand-woven carpet and tapestries reminded me of the crests of the mountains outside. Woven fabrics and charms dangled from dreamcatchers displayed on the walls.

A black tray filled with jewelry sitting on a chestnut countertop grabbed my attention. I surveyed the unique shapes and designs of necklaces and bracelets created by the Native Americans in the community, the rows of metal conjuring an array of colors and designs.

A delicate silver ring caught my eye. The oval turquoise rock in the center was unlike anything I'd ever seen. Carved above the stone were three black lines that appeared to look like a bear's claw marks—exactly the ring I saw on the woman's finger today.

I picked it out of the tray. It gradually slid down my ring finger, and I smiled, admiring its beauty.

Dad approached. "Ash, do you like that? I'll buy it for you."

He turned to the man in the black suede cowboy hat behind the counter. "Does this ring symbolize anything? Something about the Native American culture?"

The man laughed, looking down at my eyes as I waited for his response. "All of the jewelry here is part of the traditions of our tribe. This ring has meaning, but I'd rather not share it with you at this time."

I looked up at my dad's face, his playful grin directed to the man. "Oh, come on, let it out. I can tell by your face it's funny."

The clerk held up his hands in a way that said *Don't shoot the messenger.* "This ring grants the owner a great sex life. That's what this symbol means."

My body became hot, wrapped in embarrassment. I immediately wanted to crawl inside of my skin and disappear. I paused for a moment, still secretly wanting the beautiful piece of jewelry on my hand but afraid that Dad would no longer purchase it for me. But then tremendous laughter flowed out of my father's mouth and filled the room. I stood in shock, wondering what he would say next.

He shrugged his shoulders. "Well, this is the one my daughter wants. One day, very, very far away, maybe its meaning will work out for her."

Then my heart aches as I remember back in high school after he was killed. The family vacation to Arizona and that ring came back to me. I searched every jewelry box in my bedroom. I threw bulks of clothing out of drawers. Knickknacks from shelves went flying as I was convinced I'd find the ring hidden behind something. But the very special, one-of-a-kind ring that my father bought for me when I was a little girl was gone forever.

My eyes feel heavy, and I finally begin to drift into sleep, dreaming of my dad's blue eyes and that turquoise ring.

But then, in the morning, a kiss on my shoulder wakes me and I blink, strong sunlight hitting my face. I turn, pressing my lips against Eric's as our legs rub against one another under the sheets. Our noses touch and he whispers, "Good morning, fiancée."

I cover my face with my hand, shy that I can't control the immense smile. "I don't think it'll ever feel real to hear you say that. Fiancée. I'm still in shock! Seriously, I couldn't sleep last night. I kept holding up my hand, staring at this ring."

Eric pulls my hand close to his mouth, kissing my fingertips. "I knew I'd catch you off guard. I've been working on this ring for months, making sure it was perfect."

My hands press against his face. "How were you able to do it? Propose on the beach where my dad used to take me?"

His fingers trace the sharp borders of the solitaire on my hand. "All of the stories you've told me about visiting this place in the eighties with your family, it sat with me. Your best memories with him are here. I thought, how great would it be to have a piece of your dad with you on the biggest night of your life."

If this were a few months ago I'd be overwhelmed with emotion and memories of my dad. But now, there's a warm feeling in my heart. A calming and content hug, forever wrapped around my body. My mind wanders back to the woman from yesterday, with the identical silver-and-turquoise ring on her finger. What are the chances that twenty years after my father bought me that ring, I'd find someone wearing an exact duplicate on the day I was to be engaged?

Of course, there are those people, the ones who believe someone dies but their spirit comes back sending messages to loved ones to say they're okay. This thought never worked out well for me. Maybe a cynic at heart, to me it seems too good to be true—to think that Dad is with me, sharing in my blessings and sorrows. I can't allow myself to feel that comfort, petrified it'll lead to disappointment somehow. But now chills run through my body as I think of my father, knowing that he was speaking to me. My gut tells me this is certain, and I've never been more convinced of anything in my life. It is as if he were telling me: Let go of the turquoise ring. Let that woman wear it in health and happiness. It's time for a new chapter.

Now, as I admire the engagement ring that sits perfectly on my finger, I know what he means. That old ring represents my past, and this new ring is my future.

19

Unleashed

My mom's long nails tickle my spine as she pulls up the zipper of my wedding dress. I can see her reflection in the ornate golden mirror. She stands behind me, her red lips smiling. A lace corset wraps around my waist. Her hands travel downward as if blessing the embellished floral ball-gown. I stare ahead, my fingers delicately brushing the sweetheart top of the gown. Beside the mirror is a large window. Perched on the highest point of Long Island, in Oheka Castle, the bridal suite overlooks lush gardens stretching into the distance. If I look close enough, I can see the blue water of the Sound just beyond the hills.

I turn around, my mother's bronze dress glistening from the perfectly placed stones in the fabric. "Mom, thank you for planning everything. It's the most special day of my life. I never dreamed I'd have a wedding like this."

She shakes her head. "Never thank me. This is the greatest gift. To be your mother, healthy and happy, able to give my daughter away. There's no greater honor as a parent. You'll see for yourself one day."

She tilts her head to the side, and I can see, in her imagination, grandchildren running across the landscape of her mind.

Her soft hands brush through my hair, the loose curls flowing past my shoulders toward the center of my back. Her eyes squint and she blinks to hold in the tears. "You know what I thought of this morning? The game you used to play with Dad when you were a kid. When you'd pretend to be a bride. Do you remember?"

I shrug, not quite recalling. "When was this?"

"You were young, maybe eight or so. We had that large rectangular rug in the den. It was blush-colored with a thick white border around the perimeter."

I smile, suddenly remembering. I'd sneak into my parents' room and clip my mother's pearls around my neck. I would find her rouge lipstick and draw inside the thin lines of my mouth. I'd slip the oversized white satin gown from my dress-up box over my head. It came with a headband; attached was a floor-length veil made of soft jersey cotton. I'd clutch a handful of roses to my chest, the petals made of papier-mâché glued to fuzzy green pipe cleaners as the stems.

"How could I have forgotten? I'd practice walking down the aisle on the white lines of that carpet, pretending to be a bride. Daddy would tell me to walk slowly and take in the moment."

"Right, together, left," he'd say, coaching me as if we were at a sporting event.

My mom sighs. "I'd sit with Dad on the couch. I can still smell the pretzel rods he'd eat while we watched you play. Your little feet slid in my high heels. You'd stumble and trip, determined to get to the end of the aisle with them on."

She bends down, opening a black shoe box as she lifts two silver heels from the wrapping. "Something borrowed, my love." The open-toed Badgley Mischka heels are made of a sparkly fabric that reminds me of Cinderella's shoe before it was lost at the ball. My mom holds them in my direction.

I place them on the ground, sliding my feet in. I grow a few inches taller. In the standing mirror leaning on the wall, I barely recognize the woman I stare at. I've never been more strong or confident than in this moment. Not because I'm becoming a wife or because it's my wedding day. There's a warmth within my body, content with who I've become as a person. I'm grateful for my past, to have had wonderful parents, and to be on the path to one day becoming a mom myself.

Mom's eyes move toward the grandfather clock at the opposite end of the room. "It's time, Eric's waiting."

I kiss her cheek and we walk hand in hand. Greeted by a spiral staircase wrapped in ivy, we descend toward the courtyard. I hold the gathered crinoline of my gown carefully, praying it stays clean. Two French doors open, and a breeze rushes inside. Sheer ivory curtains float upward toward crown-molded ceilings and crystal chandeliers. A photographer stands several feet ahead, the clicking of the camera causing my heart to race, knowing Eric isn't far. The photographer moves awkwardly across the grass, capturing my movements. "You are one lucky bride. The weather in April can be tricky." He squints, looking up at the clouds. "Someone up there was looking out for you today, that's for sure." The sun shines down on my arms, soothing my skin from the cool air. I can't help but think, *Man, you have no idea.*

Italian Cyprus trees line pebbled pathways. Nearby fountains sprinkle water into the air that lands in a reflective pool. Perfectly trimmed hedges in mazelike formations lead me toward a white gazebo overlooking the property. My body shakes, adrenaline pulsing through my veins in anticipation. Eric's black tuxedo stands out amongst the pastel colors of the garden. The heels of my shoes tap against the wooden platform, and I've caught Eric's attention as he turns toward me. He holds out his hands and his eyes scan my body. His face shades red, just like on our first date. His lips meet mine. He then breaks away, stepping back to look at me again. "You're so beautiful."

I smile, overwhelmed with excitement. Everyone says a wedding day goes by in the blink of an eye. But I try to capture every word, each step, in hopes that they remain forever engrained in my memory. We walk the lavish grounds of the castle hand in hand. Its white stone bricks frame large windows with balconies overlooking the grounds. Spiral towers spin toward triangular roofs that sit side by side, like sentries, one wing connecting to the other.

I squeeze Eric's hand. "This place is out of a storybook. Like in medieval times, I keep waiting for the princess to step out onto the balcony, waiting for her prince to ride up on a white horse."

Eric's eyes travel up toward the castle. "Today, love, that's us." Our hands stay intertwined as we step into the castle through a back entrance. My cathedral veil follows behind, tracing my footsteps. The photographer snaps pictures. Bridesmaids and groomsmen line up. Bulky wooden doors separate the wedding party from the guests waiting inside the ballroom for the ceremony to begin. My niece Jolie runs up and down the hall high-fiving the line of family and friends behind her. The chiffon fabric of her dress shimmers in the air. Her delicate features resemble a porcelain doll come to life. Miniature pink rose petals on her headband accentuate the red ringlets that fall to her shoulders. Her infectious giggles fill the room as my brother and his wife pull her close, whispering in her ear. They hand her a small basket filled with flowers to throw down the aisle. The doors open and close. Members of the wedding party begin their walk down the aisle. The sweet sound of violin strings fills the air, and voices lightly chatter below the music.

Eric's finger rubs my hand as we inch forward, getting one step closer to the ceremony room. "It only gets better from here, Ash." His eyes travel toward the bridal attendant beside me. "Should we do a shot? Just us, to get the party started?"

My shoulders begin to feel weightless, and I wave at the lady. "Two shots of Tito's please?"

Eric's hands wrap around my waist and he bends down, gently kissing my shoulder. All of the wedding party has entered now, and it's just the two of us. Our glasses meet in the air and clink as we cheers. Eric throws back the drink. "To our future. And to my beautiful wife, I love you more every day."

Then Eric walks through the doors, and I'm alone in the large hallway. The lights are dim. My heart gallops heavy in my chest. I'm moments from walking down the aisle, and I know that this is the only time tonight that I'll have a minute to myself. Before my feet step into that room, instinctively my eyelids close and I take a deep breath. My dad's crystal blue eyes meet mine; they captivate me. Like in a trance, he speaks to me, and I feel the comfort of his voice settle in the muscles of my body. Like a flip-book of pictures through time, I feel his strong arms around my waist. The sweet smell of his shampoo seeps through my nose and absorbs in my chest. The soft touch of his finger traces my palm. His strong voice lingers in my ears, traveling down my neck and through my spine. I know he's here. And then, the doors fly open.

Right, together, left.

My mom and Joe greet me on the other side. Our arms link together in unison. I feel as though I'm floating on a cloud. Joe's infectious smile radiates around the room. He belongs here, by my side. From the day that I met Joe, he made it clear that his role in my life wasn't to be a parental figure. It was to make my mom happy. Not only did he do so with ease for fifteen years, he did so gracefully, with a presence that ensured he was there if I needed him but was never invasive. This is my way of thanking him. Holding his hand in mine, he is a part of my family.

I inch closer to Eric at the end of the aisle. I clench the bouquet of white perennials close to my chest. Their shapes, like miniature stars, huddle together as if a constellation. The stems are masked behind a white satin sash, and the smooth fabric comforts my fingers. Gold chairs line the crisp white aisle ahead, but the people that fill them are a sea of black and white. Candles flicker, guiding me toward Eric. The strings of a violin serenade me as I glide forward, as if in a dream. Beneath the chuppah, pink cherry blossoms dangle from wooden branches, showering us in plush petals. Beige and blush hydrangeas adorn chestnut arches with flowers speckled in every nook. Like a white sky, a tallit, a Jewish prayer shawl, hangs as a canopy from these branches, barely touching our heads. Its long tassels tickle my shoulders.

We stand on the raised platform, my hand meeting Eric's. His head leans down, his lips just about to touch mine. The rabbi loudly interrupts: "We haven't come to that part yet." Eric's head darts up, his face flushed in embarrassment. The guests' shoulders shake with laughter. The rabbi begins the ceremony, but his words flow in and out of my ears like the candy-coated melody of the violin. It isn't until he points upward that my attention is focused.

His fingers tap the tassels of the tallit brushing my body. "This tallit was placed around Ashley's father's shoulders when he was a bar mitzvah in 1965. Now, fifty years later, it graces this chuppah with its presence, a reminder that Jeff is with us tonight."

Eric unfolds a white piece of paper from his pocket. He swallows before taking a deep breath and then begins to read. "We've both learned early on that life is short. It's allowed us to live life to the fullest and with no regret. I thank God every day that I waited for you, that I held out for the woman I knew was out there. You love me unconditionally and completely with all of your heart. I promise to do the same and take care of you for the rest of my life."

My mom hands me my vows, and I lightly clear my throat, my body slightly trembling. "Eric, you have given me something that I didn't think existed in this world: constant stability and loyalty. I know I can go for any dream or goal, knowing that you will always be there to support me. We are meant to be together, and I truly believe our dads led us to each other. I promise to always take care of you, never let you get hungry, always leave Advil on your nightstand after a long night out, and cook for you never. Most important, I'll be by your side and love you forever." A cocktail of sniffles and giggles catches my attention, and I turn toward the guests. Many of them have their hands pressed against their cheeks, catching the tears.

Eric slips a solid gold band on a finger of my left hand, the cold metal cooling as it slides. Then I take a similar gold band, my thumb and forefinger tightly grasping it. Eric holds out his hand as he receives the ring. The rabbi has us repeat our vows aloud to one another. Then he says, "These rings were exchanged by Ashley's parents on their wedding day. Today, the bands represent a symbol of love and hope, a well wish for this newly married couple and their journey together. I now pronounce you husband and wife."

Shrieks fill the room as friends clap and shout in celebration. Eric and I look into each other's eyes. Then my body jumps up and down. I can't help but skip down the aisle! I join in with the cheers, beaming as the service comes to an end. Our hands are clasped in the air, a victorious wave to the guests. Their faces seem fuzzy, but their crystal-clear smiles captivate me, pure joy flooding from their bodies, and ours, into the open air.

Eric and I are escorted into a private study and we can't help but talk a mile a minute, reminiscing about the events that already occurred.

I point toward the room. "Did you see your crazy cousin? He showed up in jeans!"

Eric laughs. "How about your relatives from Florida? They were outside smoking a joint during the whole ceremony."

Our bellies ache with laughter.

Eric's hand goes up in the air and he stops talking. "Do you hear that? The band started, it's time!" My feet slip out of the five-inch heels and we run down the cold tiles of the black-and-white chess slate floors. We stop, the dark wooden doors closed off. We hear the lead singer shouting on the microphone inside the ballroom. Thumps of music shake the floor, and yells from the crowd boom through the adjoining rooms of the estate.

Eric and I look at each other. He grabs my hand. "It sounds like Madison Square Garden in there. Is everyone screaming for us?"

Suddenly, the doors fly open, and a sea of people have formed a circle, their arms reaching out as they shout our names. "Ladies and gentlemen, please welcome your bride and groom, Mr. and Mrs. Bisman!" Shrieks fill the air as Eric and I run inside. Faces from the past dart out at me as all of my worlds collide: childhood friends, Penn State friends, family, all separate ingredients now mixed together to create a magical evening embracing everyone who ever helped make me who I am. I dash toward the center of the crowd, grabbing the hands of family and friends. The energy of the band fuels me. The drums bang fiercely in tandem with an electric guitar. Eric and I dance at the center of the circle as swarms of bodies gather beside us, moving to the music.

Tall candelabras sit at the centers of round tables, the flames flickering. Pastel flower petals drop in tiers toward the golden tablecloths below. Eric and I remain at the center of the dance floor. I spin in circles, the floral designs on my white gown gliding in the air, revolving around my body in spectacular motion.

Songs play, from Motown to the eighties and nineties, and my feet move at a constant pace, twirling around the ballroom as if I'm a little girl. Eric and I hold hands, jumping up and down to the rhythms. The crowd around us congregates tightly together, singing along with the band.

The singer takes the stage. "I'd like everyone to take a seat and enjoy their first course. Ashley will now have her first dance with her brother, Josh." I've known since I was a teenager that I'd never have a father-daughter dance at my wedding. But at least I could have this.

I feel a warm hand on my shoulder. My brother stands behind me, his face a bit solemn. "Josh, what's wrong?"

His eyes scan the oval room as tables of people flash before his eyes. "I don't want everyone looking at me. It makes me nervous."
I can't help but laugh. "It's just a dance, relax." We begin to sway back and forth. All eyes in the room turn in our direction. I pat his shoulder. "See? It's not so bad."

Josh interrupts, "Shh . . . I want to enjoy this moment."

The minutes flash by like seconds. Before I know it, Eric and I are back to jumping around the dance floor as if it's our last night to ever party. With every spin and turn, an hour passes. Dinner leads to dessert and suddenly guests are walking around with pieces of cake and pastries.

I shake my head, looking at Eric, a grin still plastered on my face. "I can't stop dancing. I refuse to leave this dance floor!" He nods, his arms swaying to the eighties rock from the band. He pulls my body close to his. "As always, we'll be the last ones standing." I wrap my arms around him as we kiss. He lifts my body into the air and sweeps me in circles, eventually dipping me. My hair flows down to the ground.

As people toss crystal plates of chocolate crumbs on the table, they join Eric and me for the last few songs. A woman I don't know approaches me and extends her hand in my direction. "Hi, Ashley! I'm Karen, Eric's friend from University of Michigan. I wish we could have met before tonight, but unfortunately I live in Chicago now."

The familiar name crosses my mind and I greet her in a warm hug. "It's a pleasure to finally meet you. Thank you for traveling so far to come tonight."

She takes a step closer until our bodies touch. She leans forward, speaking loudly to ensure I can hear her:

"I didn't know that your dad died on 9/11."

And it's quiet now, as if the music has stopped, like I've stepped into the eye of the hurricane around me. My body momentarily becomes numb, and I instinctively take a step back. Then, like magic, the woman disappears into thin air. I feel released. Unleashed from the past, the inappropriate comments, the specter of terrorism, the reality of death, the destruction—all gone. Like my memories, they're packed in a photo album that remains closed until I, and only I, allow for it to be opened, at my own will.

Then the rhythm of the music returns, and the lead singer takes my hand, pulling Eric and me on stage. We stand among key-boardists, saxophonists, and singers, the energy of the music taking over my body as I swirl to the beat. Eric and I hold hands, our eyes never leaving each other. Band members gather around us, their vocals enticing the crowd to move forward, closer to the stage. As the last song plays, I scan the sea of faces on the dance floor that all gaze upon Eric and me. Everyone dances: Mom and Joe, Josh and Rachel, all our friends—and somewhere in the crowd too, I can feel it, is Dad.

Eric spins my body round and round, every rotation a metamor-phosis, stripping away layers of the past until, so new and so joy-ful, I emerge. Like a butterfly.

20

Three Years Later

My right shoulder throbs and I struggle to carry the heavy box filled with dirty clothes. The door creaks as I enter the laundry room in my apartment building. Steam slaps my face, stinging my eyes, and the machines suddenly feel so far away. Lint rises in the air as my box of laundry bangs on the table with a loud thud. A sharp bang against heavy metal jolts me back as I stumble from the sound. A man's hand slaps the top of a washing machine. His tan arm leads toward a lean torso in a purple NYU sweatshirt.

He grins. "Sorry, I didn't mean to startle you. It's just that my clothes are already in this machine. I'd hate for you to catch a glimpse of my boxers or something." A sarcastic tone seeps through his full lips.

I'm enthralled with the fullness in his cheeks as he smiles. The glow that his skin has. It's that X factor of youthfulness that slowly fades away through the years. I remember that time in my life. When I was free of responsibility and the only human I had to take care of was myself. "What's your name? I've seen you around the building."

The stiffness in my muscles reminds me that I've paused, and his head tilts to the side, waiting for an answer. My mind scrambles, searching for the words while trapped in a cloud of his boyish good looks and the reality that I'm married. My hand travels in the air and the chipped red polish on my nails is evidence that my priorities have changed. "I'm Ashley. Sorry, I didn't mean to take your machine."

The brush of his hand against my elbow as he collects his belongings brings chills up my back. Have I been married so long that I've forgotten how to have a casual conversation with a neighbor? Does an attractive man now make me awkward like a twelve-year-old schoolgirl? Dampness from my tank top spreads, and embarrassment sweeps through my veins.

The tight squeeze of his handshake pinches my wedding band in between my fingers.

"I'm Steve. It's nice to put a name to a face." He picks up the large box in front of me, its contents now empty of dirty laundry. "I'll toss this for you. I assume you don't need it anymore?"

The pink shade in my cheeks brightens as I smile. "That's sweet, thanks."

The pitter-patter of plastic flip-flops against the floor persists down the hall as the door slams behind him. My head peeks through the steamy window and he turns back, catching me and tossing a smile. I give myself a pretend pat on the back—the guy is obviously flirting. I can't help but think, *Yeah, baby! You've still got it.*

My fingers stick together as detergent dries between them. The machine becomes an optical illusion of colors, swooshing around in a circular motion. A bang from the entryway door against the cinderblock wall announces Steve's return. The veins in his biceps pulse as he carries my old laundry box, tossing it on the table. "It looks like there's a pack of diapers in there that you missed." His eyes dart down to the crisp white Pampers with teddy bears and stars bordering the Velcro snaps. "I figured your kid might need these."

My shoulders droop, my secret identity now uncovered. "Thanks! Appreciate it."

He walks away, talking with his back to me. "No problem, ma'am."

I stare at the numbers in the elevator in a daze as I ascend to my floor. I push open the door of my apartment, taking a moment to wipe droplets of perspiration from my chest. *Ma'am?*

A *humph* of air pushes past my lips. How is it still so hot in mid-September? My keys fly through the air and ding against a modern white entryway table. My ankles shake, sandals falling to the floor and landing on their sides. Blown-up portraits hang above my head, a reminder of times gone by. In brushed silver picture frames are images in black and white of a thin bride wrapped in lace, being dipped by a handsome groom in a tuxedo. A pond reflects the couple's carefree smiles and young love. A majestic white castle sits in the background. I swear I can still smell the arrangements of hydrangeas and roses flooding the gardens of the wedding venue.

Eric peeks his head out of the kitchen with his finger over his mouth. "Shh! I finally got her to sleep."

His eyes dart over to our sectional, and I can see Jade's body curled in a cozy ball, a delicate pink blanket draped over her feet. I tiptoe toward her, the silky caramel curls of her hair coming into focus. I lean down and slowly inhale, the smell of baby powder and lavender infiltrating my senses. My fingers trace the plush circles of her cheeks and her rosy lips.

Eric's fingers grasp my waist from behind and I jump, startled. His chin presses against my shoulder as he peers down at Jade. "Beautiful, isn't she?"

I turn around, meeting his chocolate-brown eyes. "Easy for you to say, she's your twin!"

He laughs, nodding in agreement. "This is true."

"So how was she while I was gone?"

"You know how it is with a two-year-old. Dealing with a toddler is like negotiating with a terrorist."

We engage in an awkward moment of silence and I give a reassuring smile. "Poor analogy, but I get your point."

Eric plops his body on the couch. The sun shines through the window, accentuating the salt-and-pepper strands of his hair. He points to the laundry basket in the corner of the room, which Jade has transformed into a home for her stuffed animals, all perfectly placed side by side in the bin.

"So that explains why you used the diaper box to bring the laundry downstairs. Anyway, I thought you got lost down there. Did you have another run-in with that college grad you're always saying is so cute?"

I laugh. "Yes, but the jig is up. He's discovered that I'm quite a bit older, and a mother."

I sit close beside him, and he leans forward. "What a relief. For a minute there I thought I had some competition."

Then he stands and lifts me up, throws me over his shoulder, and heads toward the bedroom. I hang down his back, my body shaking as he skips down the hall. "Babe, you're going to drop me! Put me down!"

He tosses me on the bed, my body now lost in a pile of sheets and the large duvet cover. I pick up his wrist and point to the time. "We need to get ready soon. We're going to be late."

Eric looks down at his silver watch. The engraving etched from our wedding day, *A gift to my husband, I'll love you forever*, rests against his skin. He unbuckles his belt and begins to take off his clothes.

My body jolts in the air. "What are you doing? We have to meet my family in an hour!"

"Calm down. I just want to jump in the shower."

After a quick cab ride, my feet step onto the pavement as if it were quicksand. The 9/11 museum and memorial fountain come more into focus with each step. My chest tightens as we pass rows of trees that pave the way toward the foundation of what was once Tower 1. The chatter from the large crowd rings through my ears. Like a mirage, the endless colors of their skin and clothing make me dizzy. My fingers lock tight between Eric's, and I breathe slowly, deeply. I keep telling myself, *Don't cry, not today*. I have to be strong. If not for myself, then for my daughter.

Eric's fingers interlock with Jade's, and her pink sneakers squeak against the pavement.

"You'd think this would get easier," I say, "coming here every year."

He shakes his head. "By now you know it never gets easier."

Two little girls dash toward us, their arms reaching toward Jade as they scream her name. She becomes wrapped in the smooth hands of my nieces, and the three children stay glued in a long embrace. I step toward the area where I feel at home, the sharp corner of the fountain where my dad's name is engraved. The hollow shapes of the letters leave indentations in my skin as I press my hand against the stone. I close my eyes, trusting he can hear me, see me, anything to know that I'm okay, that we are all okay.

I inhale an aromatic floral scent, and French-manicured nails begin to tickle my arm. Joe remains at my mom's other side, silent but strong, a reminder that he's here for her. "Another anniversary, another year without him." A tear rolls down her cheek.

I wrap my arm around her waist, the heat from her body now pressing against me. The peaceful trickling of the fountain is obstructed as the little girls play tag, running one after the other. Jade stumbles behind, her arms waving from side to side to keep balance. The missing spaces in her mouth are only enhanced by the white baby teeth that have just grown in. She giggles as her black patent leather shoes click against the ground. My mom grins, her eyes still moist. "He'd be proud of us. Three granddaughters, all named after him."

The J for Jeffrey carries on to Josh's two daughters, Jolie and Jordyn. And to my daughter, Jade. The swooshing of waterfalls down the walls of the fountain captivates Josh's attention. He stares into the depth of the structure and I imagine where his mind is wandering. Is it within the wide halls of the Cantor Fitzgerald offices, a hundred stories up? Or possibly his desk? In a bodyguard-like position, Rachel holds stance behind him. The crowds of people give us space, knowing that there's something different about us. We don't have a camera out. We aren't engaged in heavy conversation or looking in awe at the architecture. Perhaps it's our solemn faces, evidence enough to the public that this spot belongs to us. Our six bodies stand shoulder to shoulder as we silently stare down into the giant hole in the ground. The sounds of the giggles from our children and their innocence are the only things keeping us present, preventing our minds from wandering into an unfriendly neighborhood.

Josh turns toward the museum doors as a line begins to form. "Should we go in this time?"

My mom purses her lips. "Not with the girls. They're too little. One day, when we can explain it to them, somehow. Then we will go."

I try to imagine Jade years from now. How will I tell this to her? Get her to understand how wonderful my dad was and then what happened to him. Worst of all, in a way that doesn't make her fearful of the world. The slight wrinkles in Jade's legs warm my heart. Her baby fat is fading away as she learns to walk and run. I bend down, scoop her up, and hold her against my chest. Her fingers grab a red rose from my hand, and she rubs her nose against the petals. "Flower," she proudly yells.

I touch my father's name. "Do you see this, Jade? It's for Grandpa

Jeff. And the hollow parts of his name are for us to place flowers. So he knows we're thinking of him."

I bend down. My knees touch the ground and I prop Jade's body up on my thighs. Her delicate hands press against the letters that frame my maiden name, Goldflam. I whisper in her ear, "Let's go, Jade. Stick the stem of the rose right there, it'll fit."

The balls of her cheeks brighten as she grins, gently placing the rose down. Her soft caramel hair caresses my cheek as I whisper, "Okay, my love, now give it a kiss." Her button nose graces the top of the petals while her mouth makes a sweet sucking sound —*mwah!*

Tingles travel up my spine and I turn to Eric. "What if we aren't here for Jade one day? What if she loses one of us?"

He touches my arm. "What do we always say? If you live in fear, they win."

Jolie tugs on Josh's shirt. "Daddy, I'm hungry."

We all realize the kids have waited long enough in this heat. I turn to Mom. "It's been about an hour. What time is dinner?"

She glances at her watch. "The reservation at The Odeon is in fifteen minutes. Let's head over."

There's a salty taste as I press my fingertips against my lips. I kiss my hand and place the love on my father's name. One by one, our backs turn away and we are able to move forward.

The Odeon never seems to change through the years. We enter the dimly lit restaurant, the romantic French ambiance a refreshing change. A long bar serving fancy cocktails is graced with a happy hour crowd. My family squeezes into a small space as we wait for our table.

My mom peeks at her reflection in a small mirror behind the bar. Her eyeliner and blush have smudged and blended into a muddy color. She licks her fingers and wipes underneath her lids, clearing the makeup. "Is it too much? Going to the memorial on the anniversary every year? Maybe it's time for something different?"

"Mom, I love that we visit Dad's name. We don't come down here often. It's too hard, too much of a reminder of how he died. But on this day, it's such a wonderful way to honor him."

I nod my head toward the girls, who are sharing crayons as they draw in a coloring book, sitting quietly in a corner. "They need to know about Daddy and what our family has been through. This is the perfect way to do it. Most of all because we always end the night here, in a happier place, and we're all together."

Her cheek presses against mine. "You're right. Thank you, my baby girl."

We're escorted to a round table. Glasses of pinot grigio and dirty martinis arrive as we look over the menu, discussing who will share what and which dishes look good. Josh shouts at Eric from across the table, "Are we sharing the steak tartar again?"

Eric nods. "As always. Remember the first time I came to one of these dinners? How much we drank? How much fun we had?"

My mom chimes in, "The table next to us complained that we were too loud! When does that ever happen?"

I take a sip of wine. "That's when Eric was first introduced to our 9/11 ritual. Most people would have been intimidated. How could they not be? But he handled it all with such ease. That was one of those moments I knew he was special."

Jolie stands and nudges my shoulder. "Auntie, can you move? I want to sit next to Uncle Eric." Her soft complexion blushes as she shrugs her shoulders, embarrassed of the small crush she has.

We all laugh. Josh shakes his head. "When do you think she'll realize that Eric's family and she can't marry him?"

I wave my hand high in the air to object. "I'm not breaking the news to her." She traces Eric's fingers onto a piece of paper with an orange crayon. He sits patiently as the colored wax weaves around his skin.

"Uncle Eric, you know you have the same name as Prince Eric, Ariel's husband."

Eric squints, looking at me.

I whisper in his ear, "Ariel, the Little Mermaid."

Eric taps my shoulder, and my stomach begins to rumble. He takes my hand in his. His chair squeaks against the floor as he stands. "I'd like to get everyone's attention."

The clinking of glasses and silverware has stopped, and all eyes are on us.

"I'd like to say how special it is to be part of such a strong family. I hope we've made Jeff proud by living our lives to the fullest. And most importantly by giving the family three granddaughters that can carry on his legacy."

Parched, I gulp down the glass of water in front of me. I push out my chair, and my right hand rests on the warmness of my shirt, near my belly. "Eric and I are going to have another baby, and it's a boy!"

Shrieks from the table fill the air and arms from all angles grasp at my sides for embrace. My mom yells, running around the table, leaving burgundy lipstick stains on both Eric's cheek and my own. She breathes heavily, her hand on her chest. "It's our first grandson!"

Josh claps his hands. "Finally, we've got a boy! Maybe he'll have Daddy's eyes."

Eric adds in, "Or his business sense."

Joe raises his glass. "To baby Bisman. May he just be himself, a healthy baby."

We all raise our glasses and I lift my ice water, wishing it were something stronger.

My head rolls from side to side, the tension in my neck unraveling. My mom, once again, takes out a small oval mirror from her purse, blotting her makeup from the tears. Her right hand is raised in the air, a tissue still clenched in her grip. She sniffles. "Have you thought of names?"

A smile comes to my face. "Well, we were thinking of Jeffrey."

ACKNOWLEDGEMENTS

Jade and Austin, I hope this book helps you to learn about your Grandpa Jeff. I always knew that he loved me. But watching you grow up, I now understand the true meaning of a parent's love for their child; it's endless, unbreakable, and stronger than I can possibly put into words. You are my whole heart and my whole reason for being. From my past, understand that there will be struggle in life. It's the best learning experience and will teach you about your innermost strength and overcoming adversity. It will teach you just how fearless and brave you are. I strive every day to make your lives better and to make you proud. Know that my only wish for you is to be happy, and I will do everything possible to support you and your dreams. I love you always.

Eric, thank you for giving me a fairy-tale ending. From the moment we met, our love has been effortless. You were the steady foundation I craved in a husband, and I know that I can count on you no matter what. Thank you for being my rock but also challenging me in the best of ways to live up to my greatest potential. You give our children the perfect example of how a husband should treat his wife. How a man should treat a woman. Most importantly, how a father should love his children. Thank you for helping to provide our family with a beautiful life. I love you so much.

Mom, you believed in this story when it was just an idea in my twenty-four-year-old mind. Your confidence in me is everything that a daughter needs in a mother, and I promise to carry that on to my children. Your strength cannot begin to be measured and celebrated, as you are a truly remarkable woman. You carried our family through the toughest of times and have been a true leader, keeping us constantly united. Now it's your time for Funding for Fendi. Thank you for being a best friend and a sister. I love you.

Josh, Rachel, Jolie, and Jordyn, I came back from Boston and had a home in your apartment without question. We've seen the darkest days together and also the brightest. As a family, we've proven that we can overcome the hard times and come out smiling. It has been the biggest joy watching our children grow together to form new memories and family moments. Thank you for always being there. I love you.

Joe, you are truly an angel and one of a kind. You are an exceptional poppy and dad. You have always looked out for me and treated me like your daughter. I appreciate all that you do for me, and I love you.

Jeff Ourvan, my agent, this book would not have been possible without you. You immediately understood my story with its unconventionality and vulnerability and embraced it. You gave me the courage I needed to put my truth out into the world. You genuinely read through each chapter with excitement and constructive criticism and challenged me to take my writing to another level. Your guidance and expertise through this entire process have made the work fun, and I am so grateful.

Bisman and Resnick Family, thank you for welcoming me into the family with so much ease and grace. It's been a delight creating memories and spending time together. Eric and I value your support and love.

Thank you to the members of The WriteWorkshops, who took the time to read this work. Your feedback was crucial and invaluable in this experience. I looked forward to each and every meeting, so eager to hear your thoughts, as they were smart and interesting. I wish you the best of luck on your developing stories and can't wait to read them one day.

Jenna C, Jenna Z, Beth, and Stef, thank you for giving me endless material pertaining to girl talk and all things sex and dating. Our friendships span almost thirty years, and every decade together brings more belly-aching laughs and memories. It feels like yesterday that we were eating dinner at Parm on the Upper West Side. I mentioned a story I had begun to write and read chapter three aloud. Your smiles gave me hope that this could turn into something real and tangible. Thank you for the support. I love you and cherish our time together.

David Tabatsky, thank you for inspiring me to dust off my computer and complete my story. Meeting at Manhattan restaurants and coffee shops to eat and discuss chapters was always something I looked forward to.

Finally, I am deeply grateful to Tuesday's Children and Nicholas & Lence Communications.

ABOUT THE AUTHOR

Ashley Bisman

Ashley Bisman resides in New York with her husband Eric and their two children.

For more about CHASING BUTTERFLIES, and to contact Ashley, visit https://www.ashleybisman.com.

A portion of the proceeds from this work will be donated to Tuesday's Children. For more information about their important work, visit https://www.tuesdayschildren.org.

Made in the USA
Monee, IL
14 June 2022

98022738R10166